JAINA AND BUDDHIST RELIGIONS IN HARYANA: A STUDY

(circa 6th century B.C. to 1200 A.D.)

JAINA AND BUDDHIST RELIGIONS IN HARYANA: A STUDY

(circa 6th century B.C. to 1200 A.D.)

Rekha Phougat

Pathak Publisher and Distributors
New Delhi (INDIA)

Jaina and Buddhist Religions in Haryana: A Study
(circa 6th century B.C. to 1200 A.D.)

Author : Rekha Phougat

ISBN : 978-93-91952-40-2

Price : 1500/-

First Edition: 2023

Published by :
PATHAK PUBLISHER AND DISTRIBUTORS
E-6/33c & 34, Ground Floor, Sangam Vihar
New Delhi-110080
E-mail: pathakppd@gmail.com

Type Setting by
G. R. Sharma

Contents

देशोस्ति हरियानाख्यः पृथिव्यां स्वर्गसन्निभः

Preface

Linguistically, reference from Rigveda of '*Varuraja*', in context of Haryana is quite significant. The word *Varu* (in Vedic Sanskrit) or *Baru* (Corrupt form of Sanskrit) in Haryani or Hriani dialect derived from same, means 'full of greenery' (Bahudhanyaka). This is how, the word *Baru* grazing ( ) has been still in vogue in Haryani dialect since then.

The '*Varuraja*' (raja or rajye (reign)) has been suffixed which denotes, 'the land, area, reign) full of greenery, hence, this region of Kururastra was named Harayana (Haryana).

This land of Kurus had also the privilege of being the home of Indian spiritual thoughts. Tradition has it that the region was blessed by the teachings of Buddha, Mahavira, Guru Nanak and many others.

This is the region where eight fold ethical conduct (*angamahadharma*) of austerity (*tapes*) truth (*Satya*), forgiveness (*Ksama*), Kindness (*Daya*) purity (*Sancha*), Charity (*Dana*) yoga and continence (*Brahmacharya*) was cultivated.

Both the master, Buddha and Mahavira visited Haryana with a view to guide the people of this country whose '*Kurudharma*' became popular all over among *Sodasamahajanapadas*.

The study of Jaina and Buddhist Religions in Haryana: A study (6th Century B.C. to 1200 AD) is my thesis for the degree of Ph. D. of Kurukshetra University, Kurukshetra. It studies the Geographical background: Terrain and physical features origin and antiquity of the name and historical background in the first chapter. The second chapter is devoted to sources – literary, archaeological and accounts of foreign writers on Buddhism and Jainism. All the sources including seal and sealing, antiquarian remains and accounts related to Brahmancial, Jainism, Buddhism and others has been examined and consulted thoroughly. The third Chapter deals and contained study on growth, and development of Jainism in Haryana. The important sites related to Jainism in Haryana has been explored and visited personally by me with a view to understand and analysed the archaeological data correctly.

Similarly, I participated in excavation work at Hansi (2005) also for study of Jainism, which was once upon a time an important centre (7th – 12th Century AD). The in-situ field survey of archaeological sites helped me a lot to understand the issues minutely.

The 4th Chapter deals with growth, development and expansion of Buddhism in Haryana. An attempt has been made to study Buddhism extensively alongwith iconography, art, architecture and Buddha's visit and its influence in Haryana.

The last Chapter 5 sums up the conclusions of the study. This is thus an attempt to make a comprehensive archaeological study of the sites and the region.

It must be clarified that various hypotheses were thoroughly examined, explored and worked out during the course of the study which was extended more then three years owing to large scale out-door work and collection of the data. Some of the hypotheses developed creatively into new ideas, concepts and theories.

This work is based entirely on field work, and my sources, authorities and evidences have been mostly, the in-situ archaeological data, which is how 3 maps, 2 figures and 90 plates have been used in this thesis for illustration and authentication.

This is also why this work has taken more than three years time for completion. I may claim, modestly, that this is a pioneer work on the subject and lays the foundation in the right earnest, and I hope the future scholars of the subject will begin with it.

This Ph. D. work has been done under the guidance of Dr. Satdev who has been continuously involved with it. The Guru's debt is irreparable and I will not play truant by just paying formal thanks to him.

My heartiest thanks are also due to Dr. Dharamvir who helped me during course of exploration and excavation with sincerity, to Dr. Ranbir Singh, Prof. Arun Kesarwani and other staff members of the Deptt. of Ancient Indian History, Culture and Archaeology, Kurukshetra University, Kurukshetra.

I also thanks to Dr. P.K. Sukla of I.C.H.R., New Delhi for guidance and financial assistance and Dr. Suraj Bhan who helped me all the time. I am thankful to Librarian and staff members of KUK University, KUK Library, American Institute of Indian Studies, Gurgaon, National Museum, New Delhi, C.A.L. New Delhi, Punjab University Library, Chandigarh and various other libraries in India and the staff therein who helped me all through and all the time.

Besides this, I also thanks to staff members of Muthra Museum, Sanchi Museum, Haryana Archaeology Department Museum and many scholars in A.S.I. who helped me sincerely during my visit at various monuments in India related to Buddhism and Jainism.

Last but not least, my sincere thanks to my parents (Balwant Singh and Kamla Devi) who always inspired and cared me like anything. My younger sister Sonia and dear friend Promila has also been helpful during this mission, hence, I blessed both of them. I will not forget to appreciate the work carried out by Neeraj, Excavation Branch – II, Purana Qila, A.S.I. who took keen interest in typing work and suggested many points for the betterment of this thesis.

Rekha

Kurukshetra University, Kurukshetra

1

Introduction

Haryana is situated in the North between 27^{0} 37’ to 30^{0} 35’ latitude and between 74^{0} 28’ to 77^{0} 36’ longitude. The altitude of Haryana varies between 700 to 900 ft. above sea level. The state has been divided into four divisions for administrative purpose i.e. Ambala, Rohtak, Gurgaon, and Hisar and 19 districts, 47 sub-divisions, 67 tehsils, 45 Sub-tehsils and 116 blocks. Haryana has 81 cities and towns, 6759 villages and approximately 1,553 kms covered area by forest.

The Haryana, as one of the smallest state of India was created on 1st November, 1966[1] after bifurcation of the Punjab, a Sikh majority state. During the medieval period it was a part of Delhi Subha and the British tagged it first to the Bengal presidency (1803-1833) and later to the North West Provinces until 1858. After the mutiny the entire Haryana region was made a part of the Punjab. Today, Haryana has the vast majority of the ethnic Hindu population and language spoken therein are western Hindi comprises ‘Haryanvi’ or Hriani (the dialect of Haryana), Bangaru (that of the bangar), Jatu (the Jat speech) and Ahirwati (the Ahir speech). The Chandigarh, on linguistic border, has been made a union territory, that serves as capital of both the state i.e. Haryana and Punjab.

Haryana region had passed through many vicissitudes of history. Through, the centuries, the area remained the hub of socio-cultural developments, political and religious because of its strategic situation and geographical proximity to Delhi. The region was repeatedly devastated.

The total area of Haryana is 44,212 kms with approximate population of 21,083,000.

The boundary of this state to the north lies upto Punjab and Himachal Pradesh, Rajasthan to the west and south, the river Yamuna (Jamuna) acts as the eastern boundary between Haryana and the state of Uttaranchal and Uttar Pradesh.

The climate of Haryana is very hot in summer and markedly cold in winter. The maximum temperature recorded during the months of May and June, is as high as 49^{0}C, on the other hand, it drops to as low as 2^{0}C to 3^{0}C in January. The rainfall in Haryana is low and erratic except in parts of Karnal and Ambala districts. About 80 per cent of the rainfall occurs from July to September.

The people of Haryana have always been in the country's mainstream as it has produced the best of farmers and best of soldiers.

Geographical background:- Terrain and Physical Features

The Haryana has four main geo-graphical features:

(a) Shivalik hills.

(b) Yamuna-Ghaggar (Sarasvati) plain.

(c) Semi-desert sandy plain.

(d) Aravalli ranges.

The geo-political background – Himalayas in the north, Aravalis in the south and great desert of Rajasthan in the west-providing in fact, a gateway to the Gangitic valley has left tremendous impact on its historical and cultural growth. Geographically, the land may be called as Indo-Gangetic divides.

The East India Gazetter[2], sirsa district settlement report[3], Hissar District Gazetteer[4], and Imperial Gazetteer of India[5], all speak that area/land situated between 28^{0} 30' to 30' North and 75.45' and 76.30' east is old district Haryana. It is situated in northern part of India and river Yamuna separates this from Uttar Pradesh.

Geographically, its boundaries are bounded by the Ghaggar in North-West, Shivalik hills in the north River Yamuna in east and Aravali hills in south and Thar Desert in South-West.

Once upon a time, this region was fed by the Sarasvati and the Drishadvati, which now-a-days are seasonal rivulets and have dis-appeared or dried up completely. The seasonal rivers such as Ghaggar, Markanda, Tangri, Sahibi, Indari, Rakshi, Doham are some notable streams which flows in Haryana. Although no perennial river flows through the middle of it, yet the Yamuna flows along its eastern border, obviously, the land benefits a lot from this stream. The state presently forms the rich alluvial soil between the Yamuna and the Sutlej. This is how, this land is called as Indo-Gangetic divide. The soil formed almost of alluvium of old type containing sand, clay, silt and hard calcareous 'Kankars' except the flood-plains of the Yamuna and the Ghaggar (Khaddar).

The local couplets given below is important in terms of reference to rivers in Haryana.[6]

Akbar bandhi naa bandhi naa rivadi jaaun!
Koat tale se niklu saabi naam kahau!!
Saabi dobe maajre, leinvay bhar bhar rait!

Badro sinche jugat se dubaldhan ke khet!!
Rig benda ki sursuiti, dur-dur vikhyat!
Hariyane ki dharti ne sichen pani saat!!
Saabi, badro, mehmandi, chetang sursuiti bhan!
Naali, jamna Madhya mein basey desh Hariyana!!

The river Sahibi flows on southern border of Haryana. In ancient days remaining two rivers, were also flowing through Jhajjar, Dubaldhan majra, Bamla near Bhiwani, from Meham comes Kaushiki and joins Drishadvati which finally joins Sarasvati near Sirsa.

The Rigveda has also mention rivers of haryana[7].;

Nitva danghe vere aan prithivya:
Ilyaspade suinteve ahannam!!
Drishtvatya maanushey aapyanya sarasvatya
Re vadd agne: Didihi!!

"Hai agni sudin ki prapti ke leye gorupani prithivi ke utkrsht sthan mein tumhe ham sthapit karte hain! Agnidev tum drshdhatti (pathrili) aapgaa (alap pani vaali naali) athwa Ghgghar tatha Sarasvati nadi ke tato par niwas karney wale karamnisht maushey ke gharo mein dhanyukt hokar dipt hoyo!"

The economic prosperity was added to its strategically importance due to its three main river beds – the Drsadvati and the Yamuna with their numerous feeding channels. Thus, the religious sanctity and spiritual associations of the region largely depended on its material conditions and geopolitical' situation[8].

Sarasvati: The Sarasvati perhaps occupied once upon a time the same position and importance (Status) as have been enjoyed by the river Ganga today. She is described as the river par-excellence, and was Sinivali – the goddess of fertility, blessing the valley with abundant food supply and vegetation. She was the inspirer of good songs, promoter of all gracious thoughts and holy[9]. The Mahabharata mentions the Sarasvati, her son, sticking to her famine stricken banks and saving the Vedas when everyone else had left[10].

Similarly, river Narmada has also enjoyed holy status as described in 10th Century folk songs of 'Alah-udhal'.

'Nadi Narmada mein jal badiyon, teri badiyon re talwar' on Sarasvati was the scene of the activities of the Vedic tribes – the Bharatas, the Purus and the Kurus. The traditions pointed out by Kurus by emphasis on the growth of agriculture and cultivation of moral conduct – the twin pillars of material prosperity and spiritual elevation, Kurus laid the foundation of that type of culture which was spiritual without being unworldly and material without being avaricious (extreme greed for money or gain). It was the culture which was considered later on by the 'Manusamhita as' worthy of emulation by humanity all over the world.

The area Samantpanchac was developed by king Kuru and land became 'Bahudhanyaka'.

The king kuru in this region cultivated the eight fold ethical conduct (as angamahadharma) of austerity (tapas), truth (Satya), forgiveness (Ksama), Kindness (daya), purity (Sancha), charity (dana), yoga and continence (brahmacharya). *(Aashtangik Mar[11]).*

Origin and antiquity of the name

Haryana has been a rendezvous (regular meeting place) of various peoples and races. Its contribution to the making of the composite Indian culture has been remarkable. The region has been hailded as the 'matrix of creation in Indian mythology'. This land of Kurus had also the privilege of being the home of Indian spiritual though. Tradition has it that the region was blessed by the teaching of Buddha, Mahavira, Saikh Farid, Guru Nanak and many others.

The origin of the name of Haryana yet remains a matter of research. However the view on it are more conjectures or are based on traditions. The Imperial Gazetteer of India records that "The word Haryana is probably derived from 'Harita' (Green) as it was green land full of forest."[12]

But, there is another view that "the name Haryana is found used as an adjective of the name of 'Varuraja' in the Rigveda"[13]

Traditionally, the name of Haryana is attributed to 'Raja Harischandra' who ruled over this land in most ancient time[14]. It has also been argued that Haryana is the corrupt form of 'Dasarna'[15] (The place having ten forts). Still a different view is, that this region was previously inhabited by robbers and dacoits and it got its name from the act of robbery (Harana) on the part of these people[16]. Yet, another view is that this region derived its name from Aryans[17]. It is said that the words comes from Hari, the land of rains[18]. Another view is that the name is derived from the Abhiras <Abhirayana < Abhirana < Hirayana< Haryana[19].

Acharya Bhagwan Dev is of the view that this name has been derived from 'Hara, the Lord Mahadeva, who was worshiped by the people of this area[20]. However, the oldest and most plausible view is that this region got its name because of its being 'green land' and differently known as 'Hariyanaka', Hariala, Haritanaka, and Haribanaka[21].

Thus, nothing definitely can be said of the origin of the name of Haryana, but it was known, in ancient times, by the variants mentioned above. These variants are found in inscriptions and literary works like Badaun inscriptions of about 13th Century AD[22] Delhi Museum inscription,[23] Kumarika Khanda of Skandapurana,[24]. Palam Baoli, Bohar Inscription[25] and Bijolia Inscription[26].

This region was also known by the name of 'Sri-Kantha Janapada' and its capital was ' Sthanesvara'[27]. The present name of Haryana, however, does not seem to be older than 10th Century AD because the earliest, reference of the name i.e. Hariala is found in the Kumarika Khanda of the Skandapurana[28].

The present state of Haryana was also known, in ancient times, by various designation. The territorial names like Brahmavarta[29], Kurukshetra[30], Bahudhanyaka[31], Sarasvati[32], Kuru-Jangala[33], Hariala [34] etc. represented the territorial designations which formed part of this state in ancient times. In this context 'Yana' word is quite significant. For instance, many village names in Haryana, Rajasthan, Punjab and Uttar Pradesh suffix with 'Yana" such as *Farmana, Sisana, Dighana, Tohana, Bawana, Ulahana, Kotana, Julana, Baliyana, Gohana* so on and so forth. It suggests the extension (*vistar*) of the region or area.

The whole Haryana has so many villages namely Dhana and Dhani, Majra and Majri, Garh and Gadhi, Pur and Puri (Purva in case of U.P.), Khera and Kheri (Kalan (big) Khurd (small)) and likewise names of the localities, areas, region, extension (Prastas) were denoted respectively.

Haryana appears to be derived from the same root linguistically. Since the region was well irrigated (during ancient times) due to perennial rivers system such as Sarasvati and Drishadvati and consequently abundant greenery all around, hence, it was named Harayana.

The Dhana represents smallest settlement of a habitational unit while Thar desert region has been generally identified locally in Haryana as *Bagad*, similarly *Khader, Bangar, Nardak, Bihad, Jangal (Janghal)* etc. All these nomenclature gives an expression of the area, land, its nature and people inhabitated therein and accordingly were called *Bagadi* or *Bagado* (in case of ladies) *Khadervey* or *Khadro* or *Paharo* or *Parva* etc. In the light of such oral traditions without any ambiguity, it seems that Haryana also derived its name on account of land, people and culture.

The very name of the arid area of Hariana (Hariyana) or Haryana (Greenland) is reminiscent of the time when this was a rich and fertile tract watered by the Sarasvati and the scene of a flourishing civilization, and even in the time of Tamerlane 1398 AD (Taimur). There were sugar-cane jungles in the now waterless area around Tohana.

Historical background

The historical remains of human activity in this region can be made out from the discovery of the Palaeolithic stone tools[35] from the region of Pinjore at the foothills of the Himalaya and Firozpur Jhirka in the Aravalis.

The excavations and explorations conducted in the region have revealed that this part of the country was first occupied by the agricultural communities as early as 2500 B.C. [36]

The earliest inhabitants are generally known as the pre-Harappan Kalibangan or Siswal[37] or Sothi people. The important phase of history of this region started with the advent of Harrapan civilization, the remains of which are found from various important place like Mitathal, Banawali and Rakhigarhi[38] etc. The remains excavated and explored shows the mature Harrapan traditions in "Town planning, architecture and in art and craft."

In this region, after the decline of Harrapan civilization, a new era started with the coming of the Aryans, who followed, are known to have kindled the sacred fire on the banks of the sacred Sarasvati and Drishadvati rives in Haryana. The only artifacts that remind of their presence are historical pottery known as painted gray ware (PGW) datable to C.1100 B.C.[39] to 600 B.C. while the overlap of the Harappan and painted gray ware culture at the site like Bhagwanpura has been dated between C. 1600 B.C. to 1200 B.C[40]. So there is every possibility that the P.G.W. period associated with the later Harappans belongs to the early wave of the Aryans. The earliest known culture of the Aryans in India is depicted in the Rigveda.

In the later times, the realm of the Kurus, according to H.C. Ray Chaudhuri, seems to have been divided into three parts[41], i.e., Kuru-Jangala, Kurudesa and Kurukshetra.

However, many people of this region seem to have well received the Buddhist philosophy and religion during the time of the Mauryas as is evident by the discovery of Ashokan Delhi-Topra pillar edict[42], rock-edicts of Asoka at Delhi[43], Asokan pillar at Hissar[44], Mauryan Stupa at Chaneti[45].

The early historic period saw the emergence of sixteen great states of which Haryana formed the greater part of the Kuru Mahajanpada[46].

During the Mauryan period, this region was a part of Magadhan expire, Ashok, whose above mentioned many inscriptions and Stupas in Haryana proved that the region of present study was also a part of his kingdom. He ruled upto 232 B.C. After Ashok the Mauryan empire became weak and began to decline.

After the fall of the Mauryan Empire of which Haryana also formed a part, the curtain was downed by the foreign people like the Indo-Greeks, the Sakas and the Kusanas, But the Yaudheys – The powerful people with their capital at Rohtak[47], became independent after the fall of the Mauryas and most powerful republic emerged victorious to fall ultimately to Samudragupta, the powerful ruler of the Guptas between 325 AD to 350 AD[48].

It was during the reign of Skandagupta, that the Hunas invaded India and Haryana had remained under the Hunas for some time but soon there emerged a powerful dynasty of the Puspabhutis of Thanesar. From the epigraphical records[49] we learn that Naravardhana was the first ruler of the Vardhana where as Bana mentions pushpabhuti as the founder of this family[50] Harshavardhan (606 to 647 AD) was the greatest ruler of this region who ruled Noth-India with Thanesar (Kurukshetra District) and Kanauj as his capitals.

Harsha's reign may be considered a significant epoch in the history of Haryana for activities in the fields of politics, religion and classical warfare. After the death of Harsha a number of political changes took palace. It came under the rule of the Pratiharas, the Tomars and the Chahamana rulers. [51]

Haryana came under the Muslim rule from 12th to 18th Century AD. Haryana came under the rule of the East

Indian Company in 1803 AD. This area was transferred to the then united provinces and in 1858, after the first war of Indian Independence, this whole area was tagged with Punjab and remained as a part of Punjab till its formation, as a state of the Indian union, on Nov.1, 1966. [52]

Notes

1. Maharaj Kirishan, Tarikh-Zila Rohtak, cited by Acharya Bhagwan Dev in 'Vir Bhumi Haryana' 1965, pp 2-3.
2. The East India Gazetteer (London) 1828, Hamilton, Vol.I pp 669-70.
3. Final Reports on Settlement of Sirsa district (1879-83), pp 26-30.
4. Hissar district Gazetteer, (1904), p. 5.
5. Imperial Gazetteer of India (Provincial series of Punjab) 1908, Vol.I, p. 222.
6. These cuplets of 15th – 16th Century AD were composed by Saint Banwari Das Ratiya and Saint Harji Ram of Bawani Khera, both from Haryana, has precisely described the rivers and seasonal streams.
7. Rig. 3/23/8
8. Budha Prakash, 'Glimpses of Ancient Haryana' in Haryana Research Journal, 1966 Vd.1, Varanasi, 1970, 1972.
9. Rig. X.184.3; 30:12, AV. VII. 68.1,2,3.
10. Va.99.428-9; Mat.273.49-50.
11. Vaman Puran 26/61.
12. Imperial Gazetteer of India, Vol. XIII, P. 54.
13. Avasthi, G.C., Veda Dharatala, (Hindi); P. 779.
14. District Gazetteer Hissar, 1904, p.5.
15. Pandit Bhagvaddat, Bharatavasa ka Brihad Itihas (Hindi), Vol. II, V.S. 2017, p. 193.

16. Tarikh – I – Zillah, Rohtak, cited by Acharya Bhagwan Dev in Veer Bhumi Haryana (Hindi), 1965, pp. 2-3.
17. Munilal, Haryana to the High Road of prosperity, 1972, p.5.
18. Dharanidhara's Abhanda prapash is quoted by Shankar Lal Yadav in Haryana Pradesh ka lok Sahitya (hindi) pp. 57-58.
19. Haryana Research Journal, Vol.I, No. I, P.I, 1966.
20. Acharyan Bhagwan Dev: "Veer Bhumi Haryana", 1965, p. 34.
21. Silak Ram, 'Archaeology of Rohtak and Hissar District (Haryana), Thesis, 1972, pp. 2-4.
22. Epigraphic Indica, Vol. I, Part I, p. 65.
23. EI, Vol. I, pp. 83-95.
24. Sakand purana, i, ii, 39, 135.
25. Rajendra Lal Mitra, "Note on the palam – Baoli – Inscription, Journal of the Asiatic Society of Bengal, Vol. 43, pp. 104-110.
26. Indian Antiquary, Vol. XX, p. 133.
27. Harsacharita (ed) by parab, K.S. (Bombay), 1912, (hence forth H.C.), p. 94.
28. Skandapurana, Kumarika khanda, i. ii, 39, 135.
29. Manusmiriti :- 11, 17 The region between the two holy rivers of Sarasvati and Drishadvati was known as Brahmavarata.
30. Mahabharata :- Vanaparva, 81-84. Agrawala, V.S. shows the positin of Kurukshetra in the north of Kurujangala, with its centre at Thanesar, Kaithal and Karnal. India as known to Panini, 1953, p. 54.
31. The coins of the Yaudheyas bear the legend "Yaudheyanam bahudhannyake" J. Allan, A catalogue of the Indian coins in the British museum (1963), p. CXLIX.
32. Sharma, Darnarath, Early Chauhan Dynasties 1959, p. 201. According to Muslim writers Sarasvati of Sarsuti may be Sirsa.
33. Kurujangala according to V.S.Agrawala, comprised of Hissar, Hansi and Rohtak, India as known to Panini 1953, p. 54.

34. Sircar, D.C., Studies in the Geography of Ancient and Medieval India, 1960, p. 201.

35. Palaeolithic tools are reported from Delhi by Surjit Sinha, Main in India, Vol –38, 1958, pp. 151-154. Some early Palaeolithic tools discovered from Firozpur Sirkha are housed int the archaeological Museum, Deptt. of A.I.H. Culture and Archaeology, K.U.K. Discovery of Palaeolithic tools from pinjar also have been reported, H.D. Sankalia, Pre-history and proto. History of India and Pakistan, 1974, p.27.

36. Dr. Suraj Bhan, Excavation at Mitathal (1968) and other explorations in the Sutlej-Yamuna Divide, 1975, p.11-20, Silak Ram, op. cit., pp 90-93.

37. Dr. Suraj Bhan on the basis of the excavations at Siswal (Hissar District) calls the culture after the name of the excavated site i.e. Siswal culture.

38. Ibid., p. 18.

39. B.B. Lal, Ancient India, No. 10-11, p. 147.

40. Manmohan Kumar, Archaeology Ambala and Kurukshetra District, (Haryana) unpublished Ph.D. thesis submitted to K.U. Kurukhsetra, 1978, p. 287

41. H.C. Ray Chaudhuri, political history of Ancient India, 1953, p. 44.

42. E. Hultzch, Corbus. Inscriptionum Indicarum, Vol. I, pp. 119-37.

43. Journal of the Royal Asiatic Society of Great Britain and Ireland, 1967 pp. 96-97. (IRAS)

44. A. Cunningham, ASIR, 1873, Vol. 5, p. 140.

45. Indian archaeology, 1963-64, A review, p. 27.

46. B.N. Chaudhury, Buddhist centers in Ancient India, Calcutta, 1969, p. 31; V.N. Datta and H.A. Phadke; History of Kurukshetra, Kurukshetra, 1984, pp. 38.

47. J.F. Fleet, Carpus Inscriptionum Indiarum Vol.3, 1963, p. 8.

48. Gulshan Rai, Formation of Haryana, B.R. Publishing House, Delhi, 1987, p. 34.

49. Banskhera copper plate (EI, Vol. 4, pp. 208-II);

Madhuban copper plate (EI, Vol.I, pp 67-75);

Sonepat copper seal (C II, Vol.III, pp. 231-32).

50. Harracharita of Banu (ed) by E.B. Cowell and F.W. Thomas Thomas, London, p.100.

51. Ibid., p. 35

52. Muni Lal, Haryana – on the high road to prosperity, Vikas Publishing House, Pvt. Ltd., Delhi p. 4.

2

Sources - Literary, Archaeological and Accounts of Foreign Writers on Buddhism and Jainism

The personality of Gautam Buddha is universal and simultaneously Buddhist literature also parenetic as well as perpetual. It preserves such elements of morality and code of conduct which leds to the path of peace, penance, truth and finally *Nirvana*. The teachings of Buddha and Buddhist literature were recorded in pali language and composed in three famous Tripitakas as given below:-

1. Sutta Pitaka
2. Vinaya Pitaka
3. Abhidhamma Pitaka

The Abhidhamma Pitaka has further been divided into five parts i.e. Mahavagga, Chullavagga, Dagga and Parivarapatha etc. According to Vibhanga, Vamak and Pathan its *granthas* has been stated seven in numbers. Vinya Pitaka is like the constitution of Bodha *Sangha* and generally called code of conduct. The subject matter of this pitaka is related to misconduct of *bhikkhus* and *bhikkunis* (monks and nuns). The total number of these *granthas* are also seven.

As far as Buddhist literature is concerned Sutta pitaka may be compared with Rigveda for Buddhist. Five *granthas* has been generally included in it which are called Panch Nikaya. The names of these Nikaya's are as under:-

1. Dirgha Nikaya (Long one)
2. Majjhim Nikaya (Middle one)
3. Sanyukata Nikaya
4. Anguttara Nikaya
5. Khuddaka Nikaya

All above books contains higher knowledge of Buddhism and are considered holy particularly Anguttara and Khuddaka Nikaya. Anguttara has 2308 Suttars while Khuddaka Nikaya includes 15 *granthas*. This is one of a fine book on Buddhist literature.

Therigathas and Theragathas deals with monks and nun's story. Jatakas stories related to birth of Buddha and many other subjects are encyclopedia on Buddhist stories.

The Vinaya Pitaka and the Sutta Pitaka of the Pali canon form indispensable sources for study of Buddhism upto reign of Asoka. The third canonical basket is the Abhidamma, (higher religion) or higher subtleties of religion. This pitaka deals with the metaphysical and psychological matters. The Vinaya Pitaka (Basket of the discipline of the Sangha) is the best source of information of the Buddhist Sangha and its members. It deals mainly with rules and regulations for the guidance of Sangha and rules and instructions for the daily life of the *bhikkhus* (Monks) and *bhikkunis* (Nuns).

Mahavagga and the cullavagga of the Vinaya Pitaka throw light on many aspects of social and religious life of India and Buddhist church in the age of Buddha.

The Sutta Pitaka (collection of the doctrinal expositions) is good source of knowledge regarding religion of Buddha and activities of his followers. For literary standpoint and knowledge of Buddhism, the Suttas are best.

The contents of first four Nikayas i.e. Digha, Majjhima, Samyutta, Anguttara of the Sutta Pitaka are speeches made by Buddha himself and his eminent disciples. They are related to problems on doctrinal aspects and secular matters relating to different aspects of life in ancient India.

The Khuddaka Nikaya (Collection of the smaller pieces), fifth Nikaya of Sutta Pitaka consist of 15 treatises of diverse forms and subjects. The Sutta Nikaya (Section of discourses is a collection of poetical suttas and throw light on Indian history (early period), account of social, religious, and economic condition during Buddha's era and ethical teachings. Bhabru edict mentions, dhammapaliyayah which has been identified with a few Suttas contained in this text.

The Theragathas (songs of the elders) and the therigathas (songs of the lady elders) are collections of poem. They provide information on social condition, position of women in the society, fundamentals of Buddhism.

The Jataka (story of former birth) Bodhisattva story, shed light on many aspect of history, social, economic, religious condition, manners and customs of the people.

The Apadana, heroic deed, glorious deed, in verse refers to stories relating to glorious deed of five hundred and fifty monks and forty nuns who lived in the time of the Buddha.

The Buddhavamasa deals with legends of the 24 Buddha's who in the last 12 Kalpas seemed to have preceded Gotama Buddha. It refers to the principal events in the life of Buddha.

The Abhidamma Pitaka deals with psychological and logical matters. Among its seven texts, Kathavatthu (Subjects of discourse) which was composed by Moggaliputta Tissa, The kathavatthu is work on the development of Buddhist dogmatics during the later centuries. It deals with Buddhist sects also. The commentary on the Kathavatthuppakarana-Atthakatha gives an account of the sects and schools.

Buddhaghosa's Samantapasadika (6th Century AD) a commentary on Vinayapitaka contains information on social and religious life. The Sumangalavilasini, a commentary on Dighanikaya by Buddhaghosa deals with matters on social, religious, political life during that era.

Buddhaghosa also wrote papancasudani, (commentary on Majjhima Nikaya), Saratthappakasini (commentary on Samyutta Nikaya), Manorathapurani (on Anguttara). It refers to biographical notes on chief disciples of the Buddha. It gives an account on actual life and feelings of those women who left worldly life to follow path of the master. Besides, an account on theris life, it tells about names of chief disciples of Buddha and places where Buddha visited during the rainy season. The Dhammapadatthakatha commentary on Dhammapada), a text of the Khuddaka Nikaya.

The questions of Milinda (Milinda Panha) (1st Century AD). It deals with the conversation between Milinda and Nagasena, the Buddhist monk, on many problem of Buddhism. Milinda has been identified with the Greek King Menander (Greco - Indian Empire). This gives information on Buddhism and Menander who embraced Buddhism.

The Mahavastu, the Lalitavistara, the Buddha – carita, the Nidanakatha and the Abhiniskramana Sutra are some other biographical works. The last one is available in only

Chinese. (Translated in English by S. Beal, 1975). The Lokottaravadins of the Mahasanghikas (composed in mixed Sanskrit 1st – 2nd Century BC) text narrate the life of Buddha, according to the different traditions, for the Lokottaravadins. As a treasure-trove of the Jatakas it has a great value. Many Jatakas and Avadanas are mentioned in this text. Lalitavistara (narration of the sport (lalita), the life and work of the Buddha on earth) in mixed Sanskrit, is Mahayana texts. Asvaghosa's Buddhacarita, in Sanskrit, refers Buddha's whole life story till death. The Nidanakatha, (Pali), a biography of Buddha, Abhiniskramana Sutra by (Sanskrit) Dharmaguptas also an account of Buddha's life and his meritorious acts.

The Dipavamsa and Mahavamsa (Ceylonese chronicles) tells about the role played by Asoka regarding expansion of Buddhism particularly in Ceylon. The Dipavamsa, (4th Century AD) and Mahanama, a Buddhist monk wrote the Mahavamsa (5th –6th Century AD).

These text contain many legends and myths. The Arya-Manjusri-Mulakalpa in Sanskrit also narrates story like Purana related to Buddhism.

Two more Sanskrit works on Buddhism are Avadanasataka and Divyavadana which contains episodes relating to Asoka, his guide Upagupta, king Pushyamitra of Sunga dynasty.

Jain Sources

On Jainism, the Bhagavati – Viyaha - Pannatti or the Vyakhya – Prajnapti, commonly known as the Bhagvati Sutra, is the fifth angs. It deals with life of Mahavira. The Upasakadasa, which is the seventh anga, refers about religious and social life in ancient India. The ovavaiya Suya or the Aupapatika Sutra is regarded as the first upanga of the *Svetambara* canon. This gives an account of Mahavira's meeting with king Kunika of Champa. The Narayavaliya Suya or Nirayavali Sutra, (one upangas), the Uttaradhyayana Sutra, the Avasyaka Sutra, the Parisista-Parvan or Sthaviravali-Carita, Trisasti-Salakapurusa-Carita gives an account of Dasa-Purvins i.e. earliest Jain religious Teachers, who were still knowers of the ten Purvas, Hemacandra's Haribhadra, Bhadrabahu's Kalpasutra, the Kalkacarya – Kathanaka (Prakrit), the Katha-Kosa (Sanskrit), the Prabhavaka – caritra of Prabhacandra etc. were written by Jain teachers including Hribhadra, Santisuri, and Hemacandra etc.

Some Brahmanical works composed in Sanskrit furnish useful information. Puranas (religious literature) forms good source of information. The *Visnu, Vayu, Matsya, Brahmanda* and the *Bhagavata Puranas* are most important from the political as well as religious history of ancient India.

Arthasastra of Kautilya (249 BC to 100 AD), account left by Megasthenes, Mahabhashya of Patanjali (150 BC to 100 AD), Malavikagnimitra of Kalidasa Kathasarit-Sagara, Somadeva's work shows the influence of Buddhism in his writing. The Mudrarakshasa, the work of Visakhadatta, Rajatarangini (12h Century AD) of Kalhana are some other sources which throw light on social and political history of ancient India.

Foreign Accounts

The indigenous sources cited above are supplemented by the writings of foreigners such as Megasthenes who wrote valuable account of India. The periplus of the Erythraeam sea by an Greek navigator is very useful for economic life of Indian people in the 1st Century AD.

The Chinese travelers (Buddhist pilgrims) visited India and left valuable account about India. Fa-hien (399 AD), Sung-yun (518 AD), Hiuan Tsang (7th Century AD), I-tsing (7th Century AD) and Du-K'ong who arrived in Ki-pin in 759 AD. Through Kabul valley and Gandhara and stayed in Kashmir. All these Chinese pilgrims wrote valuable account of Buddhist India.

Alberuni, the muslim scholar who wrote Tahkik-I-Hind (1030 AD) gives valuable information on the eve of the Muslim conquest. He also mentions Kanishka-vihara at Purushpura (Peshawar).

Tibetan historian Lama Taranath (16th Century AD) gives information about Buddhism propagation in India and abroad.

All above mentioned Brahmanical, Chinese, Greeks, Tibetian and other works are very useful for study of Buddhism and Jainism at large. Necessary notes and references related to Buddhism and Jainism in Haryana has been consulted and examined carefully. In the following chapters 2 and 3, the same will be discussed separately.

Haryana in Buddhist Literature

According to the Buddhist text, it may be said that Buddhism reached Haryana through the Buddha himself. Buddhism is the third largest religion of the world . It refers to considerable, acquaintance with North-Western parts of the country uttarapatha (northern division of India), *Kashmir, Gandhara, Kamboja, Sindhu, Sovira, Madra, Kekaya, Kuru* and the city of *Taxila, Udumbara, Rohitaka,*

Kammasadhamma, Thullakotthta and *Indapatta,*. Early Buddhist literature displays that during the period of Budha, Kuru was one of the sixteen states 'Solasa Mahajanpadas'[1] (territorial divisions) and it has been referred to in the Buddhist literature several times.

According to the Mahasutsoma-Jataka[2] the extent of the Kuru kingdom was 300 leagues and included parts of western U.P. and Delhi (Indapatta or Indraprasta) which was the capital of Kuru-kingdom and it is extended over seven leagues[3]. in circumference.

It is an important part of Kuru region and Buddha is said to have visited the city. Its other parts were known as Kurukshetta and Kurujungala which included Thanesar-Kaithal-Karnal and Rohtak-Hissar districts respectively[4], Kurukshetra[5], originally a tract between the rivers Sarsvati and Darsdvati which was the chief centre of Aryan culture. From the Somanassa Jataka[6] it appears that at one time the Kurukingdom extended as far as Uttarpanchala, a town in the Kururattna with Renu as its king.

There is literary and archaeological evidence that Hastinapura, the Kuru capital, was washed away by floods during the reign of Nicaksu and the capital was shifted to Kausambi[7]. Hastinapura, however, seems to have been re-inhabited and we hear to the city Hatthinapura in Buddhist literature[8] and Buddha is said to have visited this city [9].

The Mahavastu attributes sixty thousand cities to the Kuru kingdom[10] but the specific names of places mentioned in the Buddhist literature, besides Indapatta and Hatthinipura, are only a few such as Thullakotthita, Kammasadamma, Kundi and Varanavata[11].

During the time of Buddha, though the Kuru kingdom may not have been very important politically, yet culturally it seems to have been a prominent state[12]. The Kuru king, however, find frequent mention in Buddhist literature. The dynasty which ruled at Indapatta is mentioned as belonging to the yudhitthilla gotta[13], and reference is also made several times to Dhananjaya[14] who was none else than Arjua of the epic tradition. Bodhisattva Sustsoma who belonged to the Kuru tribe made large gifts, but he got no pleasure in making such gifts as there was none among the recipients who possessed the five moral qualities[15], a necessary condition for the efficacy of such charity. During the Buddha's time, the king of Kuru was called Koravya, and his debates with the elder Ratthapala, also a scion of the noble family of Kurus, are embodied in the Ratthapala Sutta (the Buddhist text). King Koravya lived in the well-known city of Thullakotthila[16], identified with Dhankot in district Gurgaon[17]. It is so called because houses of its people had abundant grains[18].

According to the Buddhist texts, it may be said that Buddhism reached Haryana through the Buddha himself. After his enlightenment, Buddha himself had taken strenuous journey from state to state, town to town and village to village, to propagate the faith[19]. According to Mahavastu and Dighanikaya, Buddha himself converted the people of the Kuru tribe[20]. The vinaya of the Mulasarvastivadins[21] refers to Buddha's long journey along with Ananad from Hastinapura to Rohtak via Mahangra (Indraprastha) Srughna (Sugh) Brahmgram, Kalanagar[22] (Modern Kalanaur) and from there to Gandhara and Vaddiyana and back with yaksa vajrapani[23]. Rohtak, Jhajjar, Agroha, Sugh and Thanesar have been the important centers of Buddhims in Haryana.

According to the Buddhist literature, Thullakotthita and Kammasadamma or Mahakammaraddama were the two place where Buddha visited many times. The town has been named as Kalmasadamma in the Divyavadana[24] and Buddhacarita[25] and it was the famous trade centre. It is to be distinguished from culla Kammasadamma which was in Kampilla.[26] The Kuru town was perhaps much greater and has been called Mahakammasadamma[27] also. Kammasadamma was a nigma or nagara where Buddha used to stay and delivered many number of his discourses such as, Satipattana Sutta, Magandiya Sutta, Ananjasappaya Suttana, mahanidana Sutta, Mahasatipatthana Sutta etc. [28] one discourses each on Samyutta-Nikaya and Anguttara-Nikaya was also delivered here[29].

According to Buddhaghosa[30], the people of this township were full of wisdom and their food was nutritious, which was indeed a compliment to their intellectual caliber that Buddha should have preached these suttas to them[31]. The Magandiya Sutta tells us that during one of his visits to the Kuru country, the Buddha stayed in the Agnisala of Bharadvaja brahmana and converted the Brahmana Magandiya to his faith after a protracted discussion[32]. The famous nuns Nanduttara and Mittakalika also belonged to this place[33]. Kammasadamma has been identified with Kamaspur or Kumaspur (in District Meerut) [34], Kaithal[35] (50 km. South-west of Thanesar) and Kamoda (about 15 km. from Thanesar) on road to Pehowa[36]. But none of these sites has yielded any Buddhist remains or is traditionally connected with Buddhism. Its identification with above places cannot be accepted in the absence of any evidence in support of this view[37].

The town has been identified with the village Kamaspur situated on the G.T. road in Sonepat District[38]. About half a mile east of the village, evidence of a settlement of early historic period has been brought to light. A stone sculpture of Buddha was found by the villagers thereby suggesting close connection of the site with Buddhism. [39]

Thullakotthita was also a another town where Buddha visited and saty many time during his sojourns to the kuru country. Buddha delivered numerous discourses at these places[40]. Thullakotthita was the seat of the contemporary Kuru king, Kauravaya, and had a beautiful garden called Migacira, nearby. Asvaghosa gives us the Sanskrit version of the name at Sthula-kosthaka and records the initiation of Rastrapala, a saint of a local vaisaya family, by the Buddha[41]. At Thullakotthita or Sthulakosthaka Buddha converted Rastapala (a local saint of vaisya family) to Buddhism and in turn Ratthapala is described to have converted the Kuru king Kauravys and his parents to Buddhism as well as contributed some verses to Theragatha. According to the Madhuratthavilasini two other brahamans bhadrasala and Vijitamitra were initiated to Buddhism at this place.

His life story alongwith his true spirit of self-abnegation and religious discussion with king-karavya has been beautifully recorded in the Ratthapala – Sutta of the Majjhima Nikaya [42].

Ratthapala is described to have converted the Kuru king and his parents to Buddhism and as having contributed some verses to Theragatha[43]. The Madhuratthaviksini alternately spells the name of the town as Thullakatthika where the two brahamans Bhadrasala and Vijitmitra got initiation along with their family[44].

The pali version of the name which has popularly been used, however, is Thullakotthita. (Buddhaghosa has explained the town was a prosperous market-place surrounded by fertile and affluent country, plentiful in grains which kept the stores of the inhabitants always full[45].

D.C. Ahir identifies thullakotthita with Sthanesvara[46] and Bhardwaj with the twin village Thal-Kurri on the road from Ambala city to Kurukshetra via Jhansa[47], thal-kurri has a huge mound which yields painted grey ware, early historical and medieval pottery and other relics. It has thus a better claim to be identified with Thullakotthita.

Even philologically plausible, but yet to be confirmed by the discovery of Buddhist relics from the site[48].

According to Dipavamsa Buddha went to a town of the Kuru region and received alms on the banks of the Anatatta lake which he crossed[49], and the lake which is identified with the lake anyatahplaksha, located in Kurukshetra and referred to in the Satapatha Brahmana (IX. 5.1, 4) [50]. Kundi or Kundiya was another village of the Kurus, Near the village was a forest where lived.

Anganika-Bharadvaja and close by was Uggarama[51]. The village has been identified with Kundal Gram, which is situated in Sonepat (Disst.) [52]. where a high mound yielding remains of early historical period exists, and which according to local tradition is connected with the Mahabharata period. The latter suggestion seems to be probable for the village has a high mound yielding remains of early historical period.

During the Buddha's journey from Bhaddiyanagara (modern Sialkot) to Savatthi (Sravasti), Buddha is said to have passed through Anguttarapa, Apana, Kusinara and Atuma[53]. Bhaddiya-Nagara (pali) is known as Bhadramkara (Sanskrit) also[54] The Vinaya of the Mulasarvastivadins tells us that Bhadramkara was the capital of the republic of the Bhadra tribe where the Buddha had converted Mendhaka[55].

Buddhist texts also mention a town Anguttarapa which has been equated with Aggalapura, which is described to have fell on Revata's way also during his journey at the time of the second council.

This town also occurs in Tchemang's journey from Sakala to Rohitaka. The Chinese version of the name A-kia-lau-t'o may be rendered as Sanskrit Agroda or Agrodaka, mentioned in the Mahamayuri[56] and elsewhere also[57].

It has rightly been identified with modern Agroha, 22 kms. north-west of Hissar. During the historical period Agroha was an important Buddhist centre.

According to the Vinaya of the Mulasarvastivadins and Divyavadana, Buddha also visited Rohitaka and Srughana. Rohitaka was a great and prosperous city[58]. The same text narrates the story of Buddha's visit to Srughna (modern sugh near Jagadhari where he won over the Brahman Indra who boasts of having no equal in beauty, youth and learning[59].

From what has been stated above it would become clear that Lord Buddha visited Haryana on several occasions and delivered some of his most profound discourses there. The Nikayas, their commentaries and The Jatakas are our most important sources of information on the history of the spread of Buddhism in this part of India. P.C. Bagchi[60] by his patient researches, has shown that Buddha's visit to north-western India are preserved in Sanskrit, Chinese and Tibetan texts.

This further corroborates the account of the pali-literature which relates in details Buddha's visits to the land of the Kurus and his conversion of a large number of its people to his faith.

The impact of Buddhism over this region further finds support to Hiuentsiang[61], the Chinese Traveller, who in his account of Srughna (Sugh in district Yamunanagar) mentions an Asokan Supta towards the west of yamuna containing hair and nail relics of Tathagata (Buddha) at a spot where in former times the Tathagata had preached the law to convert (men), and to its right and left were stupas containing mortal remains of Buddha's famous disciples Sariputtra and Maugalaya-yana and other great arhats (Saints) [62]. This evidence of an eye witness and the existence of Stupas at Thanesar and Chaneti undoubtedly shows that the Buddhists acknowledged the importance of the region blessed as it was with the visits and discourses of the great master, for the construction of religious complexes in his memory and for further propagation of his message.

Seal and Sealings

Buddhist Seal: Buddhism was also one of the main religions of Ancient Haryana and there were a number of Stupas in many places. During the excavations conducted at Agroha the remains of a Stupa were uncovered. The same site has yielded a seal belonging to the Agroha Monastery.

1. Seal of Agroha Monastery: Shri virjanand of Gurukul Jhajjar found Terracotta seal from the ancient mound at Agroha which has the brahmi legend 'Samghasya'[63] i.e. (The real) of Agroha Samgha. During the excavation conducted at the site by the Department of Archaeology, Museum Haryana a Buddhist monastery was excavated. Most probably this seal belonged to that monastery. Seals and sealings of Buddhist establishments were

found from a number of places such as Kasia, Nalanda and Rajghat etc.[64]

2. Terracotta sealing with legend Dhamma: A Terracotta sealing with brahmi legend Dhamma, meaning Dhamma or dharma. The sealing was found at Agroha from where the remains of a Sutpa were excavated earlier. A Terracotta seal of Agroha Sangha was also found here.
3. Terracotta sealing bearing the Charanapaduka: Some seals bearing the Charanpadukas were also fund from the site thehpolar[65]. The Chananpaduka are linked with Buddhism and we may conclude that Buddhism was also prevalent during this period and people worshipped Charanpaduka of Buddha and for this purpose these sealings were made. Similar sealings were also found from a number of sites in India and nearer Haryana. Sanghal has also yielded sealing with Charanpaduka symbols[66].

NOTES

1. AnguttaraNikaya (P.T.S.) 1.213; IV.252 and 260.
   Majjhima Nikaya, Ratthapala sutta, 11.4, 2.
   Digha Nkaya, Mahasatipatthana Sutta, 11.9; maha Nidana sutta 11.2; etc.
   B.N. Chaudhary, Buddhist centers in Ancient India, Calcutta, 1969, p.31; V.N. Dutta and H.A. Phadke, History of Kurukshetra, Kurukshetra, 1989, pp.38-55.
2. V. Fausboll, the Jataka, London, 1963, No. 537.
3. Ibid, also No. 545.
4. V.S. Agrawala, India as known to Panini. Varanasi, 1963, p.54.
5. Ibid. Also see, H.A. Phadke, Haryana: Ancient and Medieval p.20.

6. The Jatak, No.444. Also see G.P. Malalasekhara, Dictionary of pali proper names, Delhi 1983, Ip. 641.
7. B.B. Lal, "Excavation at Hastinapura and other explorations in the upper Ganga and Sutlej Basins, 1950-52." Ancient India, New Delhi, Nos.10 or 11 (1954-55), pp.14.
8. G.P. Malalsekhara, Dictionary of pali proper names, Delhi, 1983, II, 1319. Bharat Singh, Upadhyaya, Buddha-kalina Bharatiya Bhugol (Hindi), prayag, V.S.2018, p.411. Also see Divyavadana (P.L. Vaidya, Darbhanga 1959) pp – 293ff;
9. Divyavadana p. 45.
10. O.P. Bhardwaj, Studies in the historical Geography of Ancient India, Delhi, 1986, p.150.
11. B.N. Raychaudhuri, Buddhist centre in Ancient India, Calcutta, 1969, pp-133-34.
12. B.C. Law, India as described in the early texts of Buddhism and Jainism, London, 1941, p.96.
13. Sutasoma Jatak is IV.361, V.457.
14. Ibid, II, 366; III, was none else than Arjuna of the epic tradition. 400; IV.450; VI. 260etc.
15. Ibid; IV. 361.
16. Ibid, 54; Thergatha commentary, II. 30
17. Silakram, Archaeology of Rohtak and Hissar Districts 9haryana), Ph. D. Thesis, 1972 (K.U.K.) p. 107.
18. B.S. Upadhyaya, Buddha Kalina Bharatiya Bhugala, Prayaag (2018), p.410.
19. D.C. Ahir, Buddhism in the Punjab, Haryana and Himachal Pradesh, Delhi, 1971, pp.11 ff.
20. Mahavastu, Calcutta ecl. Vol.II, P.564; Digha Nikaya 11.54 ff; 11.55ff; also see B.C. Law, 'Kurukshetra in Ancient India".
21. Mulasarvastivadin-vinaya, part- I, ed.S. Bagchi, Darbhanga, 1967, pp.8, 145, 173.

22. M. Winternitz, A history of Indian literature, Vol.II, Calcutta, 1933, p.232.
23. E. Frauwallner, the Earliest vinaya and the beginnings of Buddhist literature, Rome 1956, pp.31 ff.
24. Divyavadana, ed, cowell and Neill, Cambridge, pp.515 ff.
25. Buddhacarita (Ed. With Hindi tr. By S.N. Chowdhuri, Purnea, 1955)XX 1.27.
26. The Jataka, No.578 and also see Davendra Handa.
27. Ibid., No.537.
28. G.P. Malalasekera, Dictionary of pali proper names, I, P.528.
29. See above, pp.8-12, And also see D.C. Ahir, Buddhism in the Punjab, Haryana and Himachal Pradesh, New Delhi, 1971, pp.11 ff.
30. G.P. Malalasekhra, op. cit.
31. Ibid.
32. Majjhima Nikaya, II, pp. 1985 f. mayanaiya offered to Buddha his beautiful daughter magandiya in marriage but the offer was declined for obvious reason.
33. B.N. Chaudhuri, Buddhist centers in Ancient India, Calcutta, 1969, p.31. See also Therigatha commentary (Bombay University publication) pp.56-57.
34. Bharat Singh Upadhaya, Buddha-Kalina Bharatiya Bhugola (Hindi), prayaga, V.S. HS 2018, p.410.
35. D.C. Ahir, Buddhism in the Punjab, Haryana and Himachal Pradesh, New Delhi, 1971, p.14.
36. O.P. Bhardwaj (Studies in the Historical Geography of Ancient India, Delhi, 1986, p.159.)
And for above also see Davendra Handa, Heritage of Haryana II, Buddhist remains, Department of Arch and Museums, Haryana, Chandigarh, 1989, p.8.
37. Ahir, OP. cit., p.14.

38. Silak Ram, Archaeology of Rohtak and Hissar district, Ph. D. Thesis, K.U.K., 1972, pp.104-105.

39. Ibid, Also see Kamla Nehra, 'Haryana in Ancient times: cleanings from Buddhist literature'. JHS.Vol. XVI, 1984, p.1-5.

40. D.C. Ahir, Buddhism in the Punjab, Haryana and Himachal Pradesh, New Delhi, 1971, pp. 12-15.

41. Buddhacarita (Ed. With Hindi tr. By S.N. Choudhuri, Purnea, 1955) XXI. 26. In the Avadanasataka (Ed. P.L. Vaidya, Darbhanga, 1958, D.227), however, Ratthnapal has been described as Kuru kings nephew.

42. Majjhima Nikaya, No.82. (Majjhima, Tr, Horner, II, pp.250ff.

43. B.C. Law, Tribes in Ancient India, 2nd ed, Poona, 1973, p.22; Majjhima Nikaya (Ed Jagdish Kashyap, Nalanda, 1952). Vol. II, pp.281ff.

44. O.P. Bhardwaj (Studies in the Historical Geography of Ancient India, Delhi, 1986, 1986, p.157)

45. B.N. Chaudhary, Buddhist centers in Ancient India, Calcutta, 1969, p.31.

46. Ahir, OP. cit, p.15.

47. Bhardwaj, OP. cit, p. 157.

48. Silak Ram, Arch of Rohtak and Hissar districts, Unpublished thesis, K.U.K., 1972, p. 107; identified thullakottthita with Dhankot in district Gurgaon but without any evidence.

49. Dipavamsa (Ed. H. Oldeberg, London, 1879), W.43-44.

50. Datta and phadke, History of Kurukshetra, Kurukshetra, 1984, p.39.

51. B.S. Upadhaya, Buddha Kalina Bharatiya Bhugole, prayag (2018), p.140.

52. Silak Ram, Arch of Rohtak and Hissar Distt. (Haryana), Ph. D. thesis, 1972, p. 105.

53. Fordetals see J. Przyluski, Ancient peoples of the Punjab, Indian studies Calcutta, 1960, pp. a ff.

54. Divyavadana, pp.77 ff.

55. Vinayapitak, part I (Ed. S. Bagchi), Darbhanga 1967, pp.145ff.

56. Agrodake Malyadharah (Line 8) and Agrodake Munjakesah (Line70) of Mahamayuri edited by Sylvain Levi in journal Asiatique, 1915, pp.19-138.

57. Davendra Handa, "some important town of Haryana: A study of their past. Journal of Haryana studies, Kurukshetra. Vol. III (1970).pp.4-12.

58. Divyavadana, Ed. P.L. Vaidya, Darbhanga, 1959, pp 67 ff. Also see Handa (1970), Loc. Cit.

59. Ibid. p. 47.

60. P.C. Bagchi, Sino Studies, Calcutta, 1947 Mallasarvastiva vinaya, ed. S. Bagchi, Darbhanga, 1967, I.

61. Buddhist records of the western world, P. Samuel Beal, p. 187. Thomas Watters, on Yuan Chwang's Travels in India, Delhi, 1961, p.31.

62. Buddhist records of the Western World, Ir. Samuel Beal, p. 187; Thomas Watters, op cit.1.

63. Information from Shri Virjanand.

64. For the details of Buddhist seals see Thaplayal K.K. Op. cit.

65. ASIAR, 1921-22 p 46 CF Manmohan Kumar op. cit, p.307.

66. Sharma G.B. and Monmohan Kumar coins, seals and sealing from Sanghol, pl IX. B.

3

The Growth and Development of Jainism in Haryana

The origin of Jainism goes back to hoary past and recognized as older than Buddhism. In fact, Hinduism, (Sanatan Dharma) Jainism and Buddhism are the three religious faiths that have influenced human thought and life of Indian people through the ages. Jainism is very simple religion and believe that Jaina Tirthankaras, twenty four in numbers, have attained *Kaivalya* (Nirvana, moksha or salvation) and they are Jinas, having been emancipated from worldly attachments viz *vitaraga* and, therefore, originally, the worship of Jinas did not involve such rituals as '*Lepa*', '*Bhoga*' or *Prasada*, *Pushpanjali or Dipanjali* and *Arti* which are later accretions in the Jaina worship under Hindu influence. The Jina images do not live like *Saiva* and *Vaisnava* Gods and, originally no '*prana-pratistha*' was performed at the time of their consecration. Precisely, they are only '*pratika*' (symbols) and *chhavi* (glimpse) to lead to spirituality and their devotees are not supposed to be attached to them as the devotees of Vishnu *(krsna)* and Siva are to their Gods. Consequently, the sculptures of Jina Tirthankaras are static *(sthira)* and stereotyped *(jada)* depicted in '*santa*' sentiment, in detached expression *(vitaraga bhava)* in penance, artlessly[1].

Accordingly to Jainism, ultimate release from matter is, the ideal state of existence for the soul and Jains are very careful not to destroy life.

The antiquity of Jainism is very old and according to Jaina *puranas* and the *caritas*, their twenty-two Tirthankaras flourished several thousand years before Christ. P.C. Roy Choudhury thinks that "Not much research is possible in the pre-historical age as to the role Bihar played in the story of Jainism. But some of the ancient Jaina scriptures mention that Jainism had been preached in Magdha (Bihar) by *Rasabha* at the end of Stone Age and the beginning of the agriculture age. At that remote period Magadha was separated from the rest of India by *Ganga-Sagara*. The ancient history of Nepal bears this also".[2]

The discovery of seals and nude male torso of stone from Harappa have led some scholars to believe that they are Jain Tirthankaras. But, this view has not been accepted by art historian largely[3].

The last two, Tirthankaras *Parsvanatha* and *Mahavira* were historical figures. The *Mahavira* was contemporary of the Buddha. The Jains regard their Tirthankaras superior even to the Hindu Gods i.e. *Deva-deva* or *Devadi-deva* and free from the circle of Transmigration[4]. *Adinatha*, the first Tirthankar is the propounder of the Jaina religion.

Mahavira has been stated as honourable to Bimbisara and his son Ajatasatru, the king of Magadha. According to the Jains canons, Udayana, the son of Ajatasatru was also a Jain.

The *Hathigumpha* inscription[5] records that a Nanda king had taken away an image of a Jina as a trophy from Kalinga to Magadha.

A torso of a naked male figure was found at Lohanipur near Patna[6] has Mauryan polish (*Vajralep*) preserved throughout. One more sculpture from same site without polish belongs to Sunga period.

King Kharavla of Kalinga (2nd-1st Century BC) defeated king of Magadha and took back the Jina image.

During the Kushana period Jainism was flourishing in northern India.

In the 7th Century Jainism was prevalent all over India as a fully developed religion. Yuan Chwang had seen the followers of both *Digambara* and *Svetambara* sects of Jainsim at Taxila in the West and at *Vipula* in the East.

A beautiful image of Parsvanatha belonging to Vardhana period (7th Century AD) was found at Gyaraspur near Bhilsa (now in Victoria and Albert Museum, London). By the beginning of the 8th Century AD. Haribhadra Suri and many other *Acharyas* rescued Jainism and followers of the Gaccha (*Kharatra Gaccha*) founded temples at Marwar, Chittor, Marot and Nagar in Rajasthan. The Jinapati contemporary of the Chauhan King Prithviraja of Delhi and Ajmer carried the message of his teachers to all parts of Rajasthan. Jainism continued to flourish during Muslim rule also.

The Buddhist literature refers influence of Jainism in Haryana even contemporary to Buddha[7]. It appears Jainism entered Haryana along the trade route from Rajasthan.

The Yaudhayas were cultural, politically advanced and brave people who ruled from Rohtak. The folk culture of Haryana was very popular even in far off regions of the country.

The tradition of folk culture and music of Haryana is still continued unbreakable although in changed form. A

Jaina text speaks of 'the drummers of Rohtak' who attracted crowds of hundreds by their folk music. Divyadana describes the ancient town of Rohtak as fortified, thickly populated and inhabited by prosperous nobles and merchants'. The ruins of '*Khokhra kot*' are standing witness to such description. The Jain authors such as *Somadeva* and *Pushpadanta* who flourished in 10th Century A.D. **'the *Yaudhaya* country was like a ornament on earth, people having all objects, necessary for the pursuit of religion (*dharma*), material gain (*artha*), its villages were full of cattle wealth, abundance of irrigation works, well watered fields of black soil (*krsnabhumi*) settled by all the 18 categories, the people were hospitable and large hearted, ladies are beautiful and robust, live and led peaceful life without social friction; and cast remained intact, the people respected the *Varnasrama dharma*'.**

The early remains of Jainism in Haryana are scanty may be due to reason that proper archaeological survey has not been conducted so far thoroughly. The Jaina texts suggests that Jainism flourished in Haryana a little early but after 8th Century AD Haryana emerged as main centre of Jainism.

Jain centers in Haryana during ancient times

Large number of Jain sculpture in stone and bronze were discovered particularly in the southern part. Beside this, architectural parts of the temples and other antiquities has been found from many important places such as *Agroha, Hansi, Ranila (Bhiwani), Asthal-Abohar (Rohtak), Sonepat, Rohad, Badli, Kasan and Ferozpur Jhirka (Gurgaon), Rewari, Nahad, Dadri and Narnaul.* The Jain literature also refers to the importance of these places. There are various living Jain temples in most of these towns and villages mentioned above and large number of sculptures of Jain *Tirthankars* are found as a chance discovery from time to time and many of them are still under worship in these temples (Map 3/1). Apart from sculptures and architectural parts a good number of Jain manuscripts are also preserved in the temples and other research centers. Generally wall paintings are also found in some of these living temples and that too in good condition.

Mahavira and *Buddha* were contemporary and impact of Jainism in Haryana reflected at many places in Buddhist literature. Some of the scholars are of the view that Jainism have been propagated in *Agroha* region by the Jain *Archarya 'Lohacharya*[8]. But early evidences of Jain antiquity are available from Bihar, Gujarat and Rajasthan where Jainism flourished little early than Haryana. Since, Agroha is situated on ancient trade route from Rajasthan and Gujarat both, hence, possibility of *Agroha* being a fountainhead of Jainism may be ruled out.

As suggested by literary sources and other tradition of Jainism it has been observed that Mahavira, the 24th Jain Tirthankar, visited Rohtak[9] many times which was then a flourishing town. It has also been stated that in the garden of *Pudhavivadimsaya Dharma Yaksa* image was under worship in Rohtak. Jain's temples were constructed at Rohtak because this place was visited by *Mahavira* and, obviously, became Jain Centre. The sculptures of Jain tirthankars have been found from the vicinity of *Khokhra kot* but these antiquities belongs to early Rajput period.

Hansi

Ancient Ashika (Hansi) (Pls. 3/1) has been an important centre of Jainism since 1st-2nd Century AD and predominantly during 7th to 10th Century AD, owing to its situation on ancient trade route originated from *Marv* Through Gazni, Qandhar to Indraprastha via Multan, Sirsa and Rohtak. The *Jinalyas* of Hansi were regular *Chaturmas* seat of Jain *Archarya's* such as *Jinesvara Suri*, and his disciple *Jinaballabha Suri* belonging to '*Khartargacha*'. Both these Acharya's wrote many commentaries (*Tika*) and contributed literary a lot[10]. The work of these Acharyas is very important source material as far as Jainism is concerned in this region.

Be that as it may, *Digambar Jain* attained gradually higher position at Hansi and similarly *Svetambara* hold high status respectively.

A fairly large number of Jain sculptures (Tirthankars), architectural members of Jain temples such as pillars, eves and bracket have been discovered from Hansi and its neighbourhood within a radius of 25 kms.

Some contemporary and secondary sources of Jainism (Sutras) herald loudly about regular visits of many Acharya's at Hansi and this is how Hansi became an '*Atisya kshetra*' in Haryana.

During course of excavation and exploration carried out recently of this region large numbers of Jain Sculptures were discovered. I explored many villages around Hansi and found temple parts and sculptures of Jinas partly damaged and broken. On the basis of these discoveries, unequivocally, it is confirmed that during early medieval period (7th to 10th Century AD) the Rajput rulers who held sway over this region patronized and propagated Jainism. Simultaneously large number of temples were constructed at Hansi and *Ghirai* village during this period (pls.3/2). The similar picture emerged from other villages also which still yielded Jain relics scattered all around. It is noteworthy that many decorated and carved pillars, brackets of Jain temples are found reused, in Gujari Mahal at Hisar, during Khalji dynasty rule in abundance. Damaged and partly broken sculptures of Jain Tirthankars discovered from this region (area) are described as follow iconographically.

Iconography of Jain sculpture and architectural members discovered from Hansi excavation.

Large number of Jain sculptures and architectural parts of the temples have been discovered from the Hansi mound (fort) and its vicinity. The villages within a radius of 20 kms were explored by me to study the art and architecture, sculptural remains, antiquarian remains of the area and other relics of archaeological and historical importance. From time to time many scholars have found such relics of the 7th to 11th Century AD in abundance. The excavation carried out by Archaeological Survey of India during 2003 to 2005 has also revealed some broken sculptures and temple parts of the Jinalyas.

1) One broken head of a Tirthankar (Pls. 3/3), painted red was found from the trench laid outside the fort in rain-gullly. It has curly hair, elongated ears (*Mahapurusa Lakshana*) and eyes in meditative posture. The face has been depicted without any expression or feeling (*Vetraga*) and a lotus hollow behind. The chin is round, sharp nose, prominent cheeks while eye-brows are stretched like bow. It is a very good specimen of classical age and datable to 9th to 10th Century AD. The head is made of buff stone but painted red due to Sastric prescription of

red colour in case of Vasupujya Tirthankar whereas for *Bimb* red colour has been prescribed.

2) The second image of *Parsvanatha* (Pls. 3/4) was also found in excavation carved on the architectural members of a temple. The lintel portion of the stone is broken and Tirthankar *Parsvanatha* has been depicted seated in *Padmasana* posture on pedestal. The five hoods of snake are depicted behind seated Jina in a nich. It is extremely interesting piece of doorjamb where the *Parsavanatha* image has been carved in the centre of the lintel at '*Lalatbimba*'. The figure has been carved roughly and may be dated 11th Century AD. It is noteworthy that originally this doorjamb was used in Siva temple and subsequently found re-used in Jain temple at later stage. The sculptural details of both period have been found carved on same architectural part respectively.

3) A classical sculpture of Parsvanatha, (8th – 9th Century AD) (pls. 3/5) was found from Hansi and presently displayed in a temple, on Hansi – Hisar road at *Atisya Kshetra.* The *Mulanayaka* is seated on *Simhasana* flanking with 24 tirthankars on either side. *Maladhara Yugala*, attendants in Tribhanga posture, snake hoods, and *Jalabhisek* by elephants are depicted on *Parikara.* The image is in good condition and unique piece of art on buff stone.

4) An image of a seated Jain tirthankar has been found from Hansi and now preserved in a temple at Hansi town. It is carved roughly and artless. Obviously, the sculpture belongs to later period. (pls. 3/6).

5) One more panel depicting *Tritirthi* (Jina tirthankaras) has been discovered from Hansi (1962) and presently housed in the temple located on Hansi-Hisar road as referred above. It appears to be an work of 11th Century AD as evident from carvings and other details on the sculpture. In any case, this is an important piece of art work belonging to Digambara Jains and suggests that once upon a time Hansi was its centre. (pls. 3/7)

A chance discovery of Jain Bronzes from Hansi

In 1982, as usually happened in such archaeological discovery, a hoard of 58 bronze images belonging to period from 8th – 9th Century AD were found from ancient fort Hansi[11]. The Department of Archaeology, Haryana acquired this hoard and presently housed in Digambara Jain temple, Hansi. The bronze images belongs to *Svetambara* and *Digambara* sects of Jainism alongwith two Buddhist images. In fact, as stated above Hansi was one of the important centre of Jainism, obviously, these images were under regular worship before its final disposal in a big pot. I explored carefully rain-gully and find spot of the hoard and subsequently correlated structures of Rajput period found during excavation at the site. It appears that hoard was buried purposefully, may perhaps to save it from plunder or invader.

The broken stone sculptures and architectural members belonging to 8th – 10th Century AD has been discovered in excavation such as *Jains, Savite, Vishnu, Surya, Sakta* and *Dasavtara's* etc. and found scattered all around the fort. In fact, Hansi was one of the holy place and important trade centre during medieval period. The *Pratihars*, *Tomars* and

Chauhans identified Hansi fort as defence outpost and excellent stronghold to keep regular watch on ancient trade route. More precisely, Hansi, Ajmer, Bhatinda, Suman, Sumana, Lahore and a few more forts were located on borders of Hindustan and remained functional as defence post against invasions from North – West frontier.

The Jain bronzes includes *Adinatha, Mallinatha, Chandraprabha, Parsvanatha, Mahavira,* and parents of *Jinas?, Sarasvati, Buddha* and other objects. (pls. 3/8 to 13).

Devender Handa has identified this image as parents of the Jina (pls. 3/13). But, in fact, the bronze image has depicted *Neminatha* tirthankar seated above (Padmasana). *Yakshini Ambika* is holding (*Subhankar*) child on her left lap flanking with Gomed Yaksha as her consort. Both are shown seated in *Lalitasana* while six images of tirthankar's are visible on (*pitha)* pedestal in (*kayotasarga*) standing posture. Hence, without any ambiguity this is very important image of *Neminatha* from Hansi alongwith *Yaksha* and *Yakshini* as prominent *Sasana-devatas. Ambika, Chakresvari* and *Sarasvati* were held highly regarded and enjoyed status in Jainism.

The discovery of Sarasvati (goddess of learning) as *Sutradevata, vak-devata, Sarda, Bharti, Bhasa and Brahmi* and invoked in various forms in Jainism, Sarasvati is superintending deity of knowledge and learning over sixteen Mahavidyadevis.

Jainism describes knowledge as five fold: Mati[12]-Jnana or ordinary knowledge, Sruta-Jnana or knowledge from scriptures, Avadhi-Jnana or supernatural cognition, *Manahparyaya-Jnana* or knowledge from thoughts-reading and lastly, Kevala-Jnana or omniscience.

Sarasvati as Sruta-devata presided over the Sruta or the preaching of the Tirthankaras and *Kevalins*. She is invoked for dispelling the darkness of ignorance.

The Jainism texts describes that through worship of Sarasvati the devotee gets knowledge and mental qualities.

Thus, in a farley large Jain temple Srutidevi Sarasvati was installed as a presiding deity. Hence, discovery of bronze Sarasvati from Hansi suggests that Hansi may revealed big Jinalya in near future at fort or its vicinity. The Jain Acharya's at Hansi composed extremely valuable literature such as *Khartaragachhagurvavali*, and many works on religion and code of conduct.

Jainism took shape and flourished in Haryana (between 7th – 11th Century AD) as classical religion and sculptures of both the *Svetambara* and *Digambara* sects were found from many places such as *Pinjore*[13], *Kurukshetra*[14], *Sirsa*[15], *Khokharakot*[16] *(Rohtak) Asthal-Bohar*[17] *(Rohtak), Satkumbha (Sonepat), Mohanbari (Jhajjar), Aharvan, Nathel (Hisar), Binva*[18] and Ata (Gurgaon), Ranila (Bhiwani, Bheron (Ambala), and Gharonda, *Jind, Narnaul* etc. Near Bhiwani, in Baund[19] village an inscription has come to notice from a temple. It mentions about a Jinalya belonging to 11th –12th Century AD which is lying in ruins.

Pinjore

Located at Siwalik foothills near Kalka on road to Simla, Pinjore valley is an ideal location for religious ambience and attractive panoramic landscape.

Traditionally, antiquity of Pinjore is ancient and had been area of attraction for human habitation. Pinjore flourished during medieval period and temples of various religion and sects were constructed here . It is obvious that Brahmanical and Jain sculptures and architectural members of the temples are found here. It seems that *Kabira chaura* and *Gogapir* (*Gugapir*) sites were also famous for temples complex and other secular edifices which once existed there during 8th – 11th Century AD. The *Kabira chaura* site yielded 16 broken Jain sculptures and temple remains while three tirthankaras images were found lying at Gogapir mound near Rattapur, about 1 ½ kms from Pinjore. It has been observed that at Gogapir mound Brahmanical and Jain temples were built contemporaneously (8th – 11th Century AD) and demolished subsequently during 12th Century AD. This area came in contact of *Sufism* at later period and attempts were made for peace and harmony. Both Hindus as well as Muslims worshiped Gogapir (a gallant hero) accordingly.

The Jain tirthankars Adinatha and Neminatha's broken images were discovered from this place. It appears that more than one Jain temples dedicated to Adinatha were built here during classical age of Indian art alongwith beautiful sculptures enshrined therein. Adinatha images were found in large numbers and dominates the total discovery. Pinjore Jain images belongs to both sects i.e. Svetambara and Digambara respectively.

According to *Brihatsamhita* of *Varahmihira* iconography as well as iconometry of Jina bimbs are prescribed and standardized. The Sastric dicta has been followed during 8th to 11th Century AD and beautiful images were carved out faithfully.

The youthful image of Jina should have long hanging arms (*Ajanbahu*) and lustrous countenance. It should be shown naked, have Srivatsa mark on the chest and represented in *dhyana-mudra* on a lion-throne (*Simhasana*) alongwith Yaksha and Yakshinis, and eight auspicious pratiharyas.

The Jain sculptures from Pinjore confirms to the above textual description. (pls.3/14 to 24)

Besides this, architectural fragments from Pinjore shows culmination of temple architecture style and could be compared with Jains and Brahmanical temples of Delhi, Khaujraho, Gwaliar and Rajasthan built by *Tomars, Parmars, Chandelas, Chauhans and Kachchapaghatas* of Central India (8th to 11th Century AD)

Iconography of Jain Sculptures from Pinjore

It is an image of Adinatha datable to circa 9th Century AD. The hairlocks on shoulders, flanked with two-seated tirthankara's in padmasana on parikar, *Jalabhiska* by elephants, *Divya Dhavni* above the head of the tirthankar on attaining Kevalya are some iconographical depiction as a*stapriharyas*. Such features were carved around the image of the tirthankara's during classical age of Indian sculptural art. (8th – 9th Century AD)

It is another image of tirthankar with *Chhatratri*, *yugala* seated on elephants, *Devadudhambi* alongwith three images of seated tirthankar on parikara portion. One Jina image has been shown seated on top of the *Udghosaka.*

It is image of tirthankara, lower portion broken, three tirthankaras (one standing) has been depicted among *chaubishi*. The tree leaf and elephants are shown on parikara area. Srivatsa symbol has also been engraved on the chest of the tirthankara.

It is an headless seated (padmasana) image of Adinatha flanked with one chauri bearer in classical drapery and ornaments. A Srivatsa sign on chest of tirthankara is prominently visible. It is mutilated badly and could be identified only due to harilocks on shoulders.

It is another image of Adinatha, flanked with attendant, seated on Simhasana (Padmasana). The head of the Bimb had been chopped off by human Vandalism.

It is an excellently carved portion of the parikara depicting flying *gandharvas*, elephants with couple riders, maladhara yugala, *bhamandala*, *yala* throwing human beings from the mouth, *chhartratri* but without 'Bimb'.

It is an work of classical art and delicately finished. One seated tirthankar has also been shown under minimature Jinalya.

It is another view of the earlier sculpture (19) and instead of crocodile, *gaja-yala* has been shown throwing human beings from the mouth alongwith garland.

It is an bimb of a tirthankar (broken) with *bhamandala*, Asoka tree, *yugala* holding garlands and musical instruments, elephants offering water with pots, *chhatratri* and musician playing with drum (*devadudhambi*). The image has been damaged badly. The eye-brows are stretched like bow, curly hair, and face in *Santa* mudra without any expression (*vetrage bhav*).

It is leg portion of a seated tirthankara in padmasana posture on *Simha – gajasana* pedestal. It has been broken ruthlessly.

It is also image of padmasana Jina flanked with two flasks bearer on either side. Srivatsa symbol has been shown brightly.

It is an image of a tirthankar in *Kayotasarga* (standing) posture. The sculpture belongs to classical age (8th – 10th Century AD) and beautifully finished. *Kati-Kachchani* on

Waist, Srivatsa on chest without any ambiguity suggests that the bimb was enshrined in a Svetambara Jain temple at Pinjore during medieval period when Tomars and Chauhans were the masters and held sway over this region more than 4th centuries, guarded and protected Hindustan from Muslim invasions faithfully.

It is ample clear from above discussion that like Hansi, Pinjor was also an important Jain centre where both *Svetambara* and *Digamabra* sects lived together in complete harmony and peace alongwith Brahmanical religious. In fact, defeat of Prithiviraja at battlefield of Taraori in 1992 thrown open gates of India to Islamic invasion which altogether influenced Indian culture and people in its own way.

Asthal-Abohar (Bohar)

Rohidya identified as Rohtak has been found mentioned in Jaina texts. The Dharma yaksha established worship place in one of the garden at Rohtak and Mahavira himself visited this city several times. In fact, Asthal-Abohar (Bohar), *Khokhara-kot* (ancient mound at Rohtak) and *Brahmanvas* village near Rohtak are three important places as far as archaeological remains of Jainism and Buddhism are concerned. All these places were situated on ancient trade route and not so far away from capital city Indrprastha. Saivism was popular dharma in this region and subsequently during 8th – 11th Century AD, *Nath cult* (one form of Saivism) flourished at Asthal-Abohar under patronage of *Machander Nath* and *Gorakh Nath*. The region became famous on account of religious discourses and experiment with truth.

The Jain tirthankara's images have been found from Asthal-Bohar and village Majra located in its vicinity.

All these images are datable to 8th –11th Century AD and iconographically masterpieces of Indian art. Such discovery suggests that once upon a time, precisely, during Rajput rule Asthal-Bohar became important centre of Jianism. Jain texts like *Kalpa Sutra, Pauamchariya, Angavijja, Vasudevahindi*, etc. were composed in this region. Since, Hansi was much important place of Jainism during this period, however, Jinalyas were constructed at Asthal-Bohar also owing to its situation near capital of the empire. From time to time, Jain tirthankara's images have come to light during exploration and a few of them are described as follow.

Iconography of Jain images from Asthal-Bohar and Majra village (pls. 3/25 –35)

It is an image of seated tirthankara (padmasana) with parikar. The symbol (*Lanchana*) *conch* has been depicted on asana portion. Maladhara flying couples, elephants with rider for *Jalabhiseka*, *bhamandala*, Asoka tree, *trichhatra* and drummer are depicted on parikera area. It is an image of *Neminatha*, 22nd tirthankar. The whole sculpture has been tastefully carved and datable to 8th Century AD.

It is an extremely finished image of Parsvanatha in padmasana posture on Simhasana. The Srivatsa symbol on chest , flask bearer on either side, two flying couple holding garlands, trichhatra above the snake hood, elephants with rider and two standing tirthankaras on parikara area makes it an image of the classical work of art. Personification of Naga and Nagini on hanging cover portion over asana has been carefully carved. In any case, the image belongs to 9th Century AD and once enshrined in very big Jinalya at Asthal-Bohar.

It is an image of Parsvanatha in (*Kayotasarga*) standing posture, partly damaged, belongs to *Svetambara* sect of Jainism from toe to head it has been carved and depicting *astapraharyas* such as, celestial music, flying gandharva, elephants performing *Jalabhisek* in graceful manner. The coils of snake are visible on parikara area also. This bimb also belongs of classical age.

It is similar type of Parsvanatha image in standing posture with all elements of Indian art on parikara portion. The sculpture may be dated between 10th Century AD and perhaps enshrined once in Jain temple at Asthal-Bohar.

It is bust of tirthankar having Srivatsa symbol on chest and eye-brows stretched like bow. The nose has been damged completely. It also belongs to 9th Century AD.

The sculptural wealth and some architectural members, richly carved on buff and red sand stone without any ambiguity suggests that Asthal-Bohar was very important Jain centre of Svetambara and Digambra sects. The large Jain temples were raised here to preside such independent images of tirthankaras. These images were enshrined in Jain localities (Basti) as generally found in other site/places like Fatehpur Sikri.

As discussed above, two images of Parasvanatha carved on buff colured red sand stone were discovered from *Khokhra-kot* area presently known as *Majra* village. These sculptures belongs to 9th –10th Century AD and are beautifully finished. Incongraphically, the images fully responds to Sastric dicta which refers how Jina's images should have been created. It appears that a few Jain temples existed at Rohtak also and these images were enshrined therein as Mulanayaka or presiding deity. The Jain Basti of

Asthal-Bohar and Rohtak patronized both Svetambara and Digambara sect and Acharya's of Hansi guided and inspired people about Jina teachings, penance and finally led them to attain Kevalya. The sculptures are described below according to iconography and Jain texts:-

1) It is beautiful image of standing Parsvanatha with one hand broken. It belongs to Svetambara sect. Mulanayaka has shadow of seven headed snake hoods with *astaprabaryas* on parikara portion. The sculpture belongs to classical age. It has been observed that Majra, Asthal-Bohar, Hansi and many other sites in Haryana and Fatehpur Sikri and Souripur in U.P. yielded large number of Parsvanatha images which was held very popular tirthankara in this region.

2) It is an image of seated *Parsvantha* with fully carved parikara portion. The sculpture has been finished on buff colour stone and may be assigned to 10th Century AD. It has been noticed that earlier tirthankaras images were carved without parikara feature and artlessly. In fact, the influence of Hindu and Buddhist images inspired Jaina art also to flourish freely during classical age of Indian art.

Be that as it may, Rohtak and Asthal-Bohar had played very important role as far as Jain art and architecture is concerned in Haryana. In case, this region is extensively explored and sites are excavated horizontally, hoary past of Jainism and Buddhism may come to light, which is lying buried under several mounds in this area.

Ranila (Bhiwani)

Ranila has yielded two important jain images carved on buff coloured red sand stone. One sculpture has been identified as Adinatha, 1st tirthankar and second image is of *Chakaresvari*, an Yakshini of Jina. Both the images belongs to 9th – 10th Century AD and finished tastefully. In fact, Ranila was also a important Jain centre owing to its location on trade route from Gujarat which was by and large under Jainism influence and teachings.

It is an image of Chakresvari, yakshini of Adinatha. The Yakshini has been depicted seated in Lalitasana on Garuda with multiple hands holdings various attributes. Two female attendants with folded hands are visible on either side, while seated Jina image above the head of *Chakresvari* has been carved on parikara area. Flying *Maladhara Gandhrva's* are also depicted. She is holding Chakra on first finger of both hands. *Chakresvari* has been regarded highly venerated Yakshini in Jainism and was under regular worship by *Svetambara* and *Digambara* both.

It is an image of Adinatha complete in all respect and datable to 10th Century AD. It is an classical sculpture extremely beautiful and richly carved. All the 24 tirthankaras has been depicted seated and standing posture on parikara portion. The symbol (*Lanchana*) bull below *Simhasana*, seated Yaksa, flasks bearer, flying couple holding garlands, Asoka tree leafs, trichhatra, elephants and other *apraharyas* according to *Sastric* requirement has been depicted on the image. *Mulanayaka* has *Srivats* on chest carved in fully evolved form.

The Jain relics of Ranila suggests that Adinatha images was installed as presiding deity in a fairly large Jinalya while

Chakresvari also remained under worship independently. Ranila flourished as important Jain centre during medieval period. The Tomars and Chauhans rulers patronized Jainism and extended royal support to Jain Acharya's freely.

Jind

An image of Adinatha has been found from Jind which belongs to classical era. The *Mulanayaka* is seated on *Simhasana* covered with lotus design cloth. Bull as symbol below, flanked with Yaksa and Yaksini and two flasks bearer in Tribhanga posture, flying gandharva, elephants and bhamandala are noteworthy features on the parikara area. The singular discovery of Adinatha image from Jind without any doubt suggests that Jind also played important role as far as Jainism is concerned in Haryana. Since, Hansi owing to its location only 42 kms from Jind was a nucleus region of Jainism, hence Jind also had some Jinalya to enshrined such classical images.

Narnaul

A rare and classical period image of Mallinatha, seated on Simhasana was found from Narnaul. It is such an image which placed Narnaul on important archaeological and historical map. Some scholars of Jainism do not believe that Mallinath who had been stated as female, attained Kevalya and included in the list of tirthankaras. Be that as it may, it is an image of Mallinatha depicting Yaksa and Yaksini seated below, Kalasa as Lanchana (symbol) two flasks bearer, flying gandharva couples, elephants pouring water, trichhatra and many other *apraharyas* mentioned in Jain texts. The one side of chest has been depicted developed with Srivatsa symbol over it.

It seems, Narnaul was also important Jain centre and situated enrute from Gujarat to Haryana. The singular discovery of Mallinatha from Narnaul throws lime light on history and archaeology of Haryana in relation to Jainism.

Badhara (Bhiwani)

Two bronze images of *Mahavira* and *Parsvantha* discovered from Badhara are similarly important jain relics as Mallinatha from Narnaul. Although, both the sculptures were under worship in Jain temple and are datable to 11th –12th Century AD. The important features as suggested in Jain texts have been depicted faithfully which makes them unique. The discovery from Badhara shows that Jainism continued to flourished during Sultanate period also. (Pls. 3/36 and 37) are described as below:-

1) Parsvanatha image of bronze belonging to 12th Century AD.

2) Mahavira bronze image datable to Circa 11th –12th Century AD.

The archaeological survey may bring to light a few more Jain relics from Badhara in future, if careful operation of exploration work is taken up.

Thanesar

Thanesar was once very important capital city (7th Century AD) and hub of religious activities. Numerious Brahmanical Buddhist and Jain temples were erected on holy land of it. The ruins of ancient city are still scattered in a very vast area. Like Buddhist, Jains also preach Jainism and non-violence here. A broken head of a tirthankar has been discovered from Thanesar. The capital from Thanesar was shifted to

Kanauj by Harshavardhan. Harsha was a great *Chakravarti* king and he allowed all religions to grow and flourish freely in complete harmony. In any case, the *Nirgranthies* (Jains) also preached Jainism at Thanesar being a commercial and religious township on ancient trade route from Lahore and Puruaspur. Jains were far ahead as far as worship of *chaturvistirhant* is concerned in comparison to Buddhism and Brahman's.

Agroha

The remains of a Jain temple were discovered from Agroha in form of a torana architrave of the Parikara portion of a tirthankar image. The relief may be assigned to 10th –11th Century AD and belongs to classical age when beautiful sculptures were produced in Indian art. Agroha was one of the important centre where Buddhism as well as Jainism spread simultaneously. Since, this place was a centre of commerce and trade and the traders even from far away places passed through Agroha, obviously, in charity a lot was contributed by them and donations given to religious shrines.

Binva, Ata, (Gurgaon Distt.) Ahravan, Narhal, Sirsa, Nagram and Somerawala (Sirsa Distt.)

All these places have yielded architectural parts and broken images of Jaina tirthankaras and in some cases *Sasandevi's* of Jinas. The relics belongs to 8th to 10th Century AD and are of immense archaeological interest for the standpoint of Jainism study in Haryana. It has been observed by me during course of exploration of above cited area that, if, scientific and planned survey is carried out then more relics will come to light and study in the field may be advanced further.

Ghronda

A unique discovery of a *Sarvatabhadra* image dateable to C 11th Century AD depicting seated tirthankaras, in four cardinal directions have been made from Ghronda village. Such images were made according to Jain Sutra's for the occasion when Jina's delivered first speech after attaining Kevalyas. Diparnva mentions in particular about the place, and such ceremony held on this occasion . Any way, such images are rare and from Ghronda one has come to the notice. Beside this, an image of *Mahavira* was found installed in a temple presently at village Bheron near Shahjadpur on Chandigarh road. It is surprised how, even still tradition survived and image is under regular worship by devotee.

The Jain sculptures from Jhajjar Museum and Kurukshetra university collections

Many sculptures (broken) and pieces of architectural parts has been found from time to time by scholars, and presently housed in the museum collection. These relics belongs to 9th – 11th Century AD, Iconographically, each one is being described as below (pls. 3/38-43).

It is a broken piece of a complete image of parsvanatha depicting two seated Jinas on either side. The flying gandharva's are visible over snake hood.

It is an image of tirthankar'a in *Kayotasarga* posture with partly broken hands and legs. It belongs to *Digambara* sect. Srivatsa symbol is sharp on chest.

It is a part (broken) of parikara depicting *Bhamandala*, tree leaf, elephant with rider and holding pot for *Jalabhisek*, flying gandharva and celestial music by pair of musicians. The eight apraharya's are shown faithfully on the image and which is datable to C 10th Century AD.

It is an image of seated *Mallinatha* under tree (as represented by two leaf) on Simhasana. The (Kalasa) pot as lanchana of the tirthankar has been carved below. In fact, it is not Mulanayaka but Chaturvisa Jina image as generally carved on parikara portion.

It is a headless image of seated tirthankar on *Simhasana*. One standing tirthankar has also been depicted flanking with on left hand side. Srivatsa symbol carved on chest is beautiful. The image belongs to 10th –11th Century AD and perhaps damaged (as the head chopped off) subsequently.

It is a broken portion of parikara detached from big size image of tirthankar and seems to be enshrined as presiding deity in a Jinalya. The riders holding pot on elephant, and couples in flying posture above have been carved faithfully. One seated Jina flanked by two standing tirthankara's on either side in a miniature shrine is classical work of art and gives an idea about shape and size of original image. The Makarayala at end is also typical.

Stylistically it belongs to 10th Century AD when masterpieces of artwork were carved particularly in North India. The close up view of the images (pl. 44) clearly shows how carefully such sculptures were produced by the artisans.

Jain religion, art and architecture originated from the land of Bihar and expanded all over India. Haryana was also no exception for Jainism. The Jain images found in Haryana are similar and contemporary to the sculptures discovered at Fatehpur Sikiri, Sauripur, Rajasthan and Gujrat. Although, Buddhism and Jainism were contemporary but Jain religion could reach within India only, while Buddhism spread in outside world also. Rajasthan, Gujrat, Malwa and Bihar were important centre of Jainism and appears that in Haryana it penetrated from both sides. By the close of 8th Century AD, Shankara Acharya, adversely effected Jainism as well as Buddhism and people turned towards Hinduism consequently. Yuan Chwang has described that in Haryana Jain believers were living at various places. The Jainism also could not sustained in its original form like Buddhism and divided in two branches i.e. *Svetambara* and *Digambara* and further many more such as 22 Tola and Terapanthi. The local acharyas were used to called *Yatis* and inside them also *Gachcha's* were followed like *Badragachcha, Khartaragachacha, Rudragachcha, Bhattaraka* etc. *Uttaradhayana Sutra*, a Jain text, mention about a city called Isukara (Hisar) which has been stated centre of Jainism. The literature fully corroborates with archaeological data because Jain sculpture were found from Hisar region in abundance. In 16th Century *Nemichand* Jain composed *gandas* Sutra in Sirsa. Similarly, Jain acharya Laxminiwas from sirsa composed Sisya-Hitesani, a commentary in Sanskrit during 1556 AD This text was later on handed over to Department of manuscript, Kurukshetra university by Liladhar Dukhi from Sirsa.

The Jain sculptures (stone and bronze) has also been reported from Gohana, Sonepat, Panipat and Sandhora.

In comparison to Buddhism, antiquity, (paintings in temples, stone and bronze images and manuscripts) of Jain religion are still preserved in many living temples and private collections. In case, village-to-village survey and documentation of archaeological and historical data is taken up extensively, entirely different picture may emerged as far as study of Jainism and Buddhism is concerned in Haryana.

NOTES

1. Sharma D.V., 'Archaeology of Fatehpur Sikri', unp. 2005.
2. Roy Chaudhury, P.C., 'Jainism in Bihar, p. 7.
3. V.S. Agrawala, Indian Art, pp 21-22.
4. B.N. Sharma, Jaina Images, (Hindi, Ed.) p.2.
5. Epigraphia Indica, XX, pp. 72ff.
6. B.N. Sharma, Jaina Images, pp.1.
7. Paramathadipani, theragatha, Bombay, Unpub., pp.56-57.
8. J.C. Jain, Life in Ancient India as depicted in Jain canons, Bombay, 1947, p.316 fn 995.
9. Ibid.
10. Suksmarthasiddhanta richara Sara Sadasiti, Sarthastaka, Pindavisuddi, Pansadhavidhi, Samghapatlaka, Dharmasiksa, etc.
11. Devendra Handa; Jaina Bronzes from Hansi, 2002.
12. U.P. Shah, Iconography of Jaina Sarasvati
13. U.V. Singh, Pinjore sculptures, 1977, pp. 16-20.
14. Kurukshetra University Museum Collection.
15. Ibid.
16. Marg, p.12.
17. Silak Ram, Archaeology of Rohtak and Hissar Distt., Ph.D. Thesis, p.310.
18. D.S. Punia, Archaeology of Mahendergarh and gurgaon Distt., 1976, MS Ph. D. thesis, p.69-70, 81.
19. Man Mohan Singh's information in person.

Appendix-A

Eight Jain Pratiharyas

अशोकवृक्षः सुरपुष्प वृष्टि दिव्य ध्वनिश्चामरमासनं च ।

भामण्डलं दुन्दुभिराछत्रं अष्ट प्रतिहार्याणि जिनेश्वराणाम ।।[1]

The following eight '*Pratiharya's* are prescribed to be depicted in *murti-rupa* on the *parikara* of the *Jina-tirthankaras*:

1. Asoka tree
2. Surya-Puspa-vrsti (Gods showering flowers)
3. Divya-dhvani (divine sound symbolized by sankya = conchshell)
4. Chawara (fly-whisker bearses)
5. *Asana* (*simhasana*, seat or throne)
6. Bha-mandala (Prabha-mandala, halo)
7. *Dundubhi* (Celestial music)
8. Chhatra (Parasol)

Obviously, these are *divine* or royal *symbols*, with which *jinas* were invested.

---

1 JD, pp. 58, 178.

Appendix – B

Eight Jaina Asta-Mangalas

(Eight auspicious symbols)

स्वस्तिकं नंद्यावर्त च दर्पणं युग्ममत्स्यघटम्

श्रीवत्सं च भद्रासनं वर्धमानाष्ट मगंलम् ।।[2]

The following eight auspicious symbols are prescribed to be depicted in the Jaina art:

1. *Swastika*
2. *Nandyavarta*
3. *Darpana* (Mirror)
4. *Yugma-Matsya* (Mina-Mithuna)
5. *Ghata* (kalasa, Purna-Kumbha)
6. *Srivatsa*
7. *Bhadrasana* (*Asana*)
8. *Vardhamana*

2 JD. p. 176

Appendix - C

Rupamandana has given a description of 24 Tirthankaras their emblems, Yaksa and Yaksini figures.

No.	*Name*	*Colour*	*Emblem*	*Yaksa*	*Yaksini*
1.	Risabha	Golden	Bull	Gomukh	Chakresvari
2.	Ajita	Golden	Elephant	Mahayaksa	Ajitabala
3.	Sambhava	Golden	Horse	Trimukha	Duritari
4.	Abhinandana	Golden	Monkey	Yaksanayaka	Kalika
5.	Sumati	Golden	Curlew	Tumbaru	Mahakali
6.	Padmaprabha	Red	Lotus	Kusuma	Syama
7.	Suparsva	Golden	Svastika	Matanga	Santa
8.	Chandraprabha	Dark	Moon	Vijaya	Bhrikuti
9.	Suvidha	Golden	Makara	Jaya	Sutarika
10.	Sitala	Golden	Srivatsa	Brahma	Asoka
11.	Sreyamsa	Golden	Rhinoceros	Takseta	Manavi
12.	Vasupujya	Red	Buffalo	Kumaara	Candi (Chandi)
13.	Vimala	Golden	Boar	Sanmukha	Vidita
14.	Ananta	Golden	Hawk	Patala	Ankusi
15.	Dharma	Golden	Thunderbolt	Kinnara	Kandarpi
16.	Santi	Golden	Deer	Garuda	Nirvani
17.	Kuntha	Golden	Goat	Gandharva	Bala
18.	Ara	Golden	Nandiavarta	Yakseta	Dharini
19.	Malli	Blue	Pot	Kubera	Dharnapriya
20.	Muni	Black	Tortoise	Varuna	Nadarakta
21.	Suvrata	Golden	Blue lotus	Bhrkuti	Gandharva
22.	Nemi	Black	Conch	Gomedha	Ambika
23.	Parsva	Blue	Serpent	Parsva	Padmavati
24.	Mahavira	Golden	Lion	Matanga	Siddayika

Fourteen dreams in Jainism

Eight auspicious signs in Jainism

Lanchana's of the Jina

Map 3/1 Jain Sites in Haryana

Pls. 3/1 A view of Hansi Fort

Pls. 3/2 Uma – Maheswar Hansi Region

Pls. 3/3 Tirthankar Head, Hansi

Pls. 3/4 Parsvanatha Tirthankar, Hansi

Pls. 3/5 Parsvanatha Image, Hansi (Atisyakshetra)

Pls. 3/6 Unidentified Tirthankar, Hansi (Atsiyakshetra)

Pls. 3/7 Tritirthi Panel, Hansi

Pls. 3/8 Parsvanatha with Yaksa & Yaksini, Bronze, Hansi

Pls. 3/9 Parsvanatha with Trітirthi, Yaksa & Yaksini, Bronze, Hansi

Pls. 3/10 Tritirthika of Parsvanatha, Bronze, Hansi

Pls. 3/11 Mahavira, Bronze, Hansi

Pls. 3/12 Mahavira, Bronze, Hansi

Pls. 3/13 Neminatha with Yaksa & Yaksini, Bronze, Hansi

Pls. 3/14 Adinatha, Pinjore

Pls. 3/15 Tirthankar with Parikar, Pinjore

Pls. 3/16 Tirthankar with Parikar, Pinjore

Pls. 3/17 Adinatha , Pinjore

Pls. 3/18 Adinatha , Pinjore

Pls. 3/19 Parikara Portion , Pinjore

Pls. 3/20 Another view of the above, Pinjore

Pls. 3/21 Tirthankar,, Pinjore

Pls. 3/22 Seated Trithankar, Pinjore

Pls. 3/23 Seated Trithankar, Pinjore

Pls. 3/24 Standing Trithankar, Pinjore

Pls. 3/25 Neminatha, Asthal Bohar

Pls. 3/26 Parsvanatha, Asthal Bohar

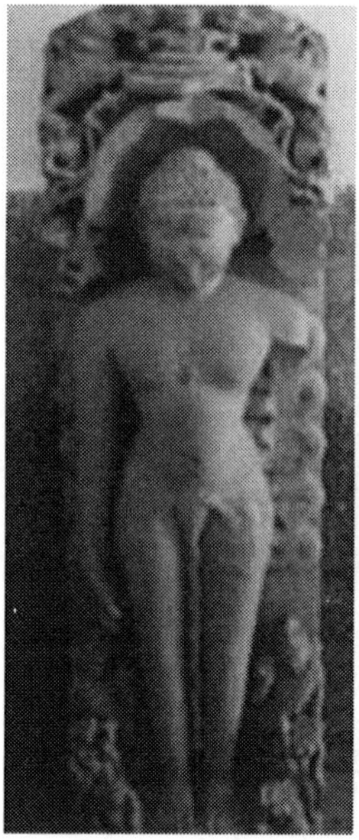

Pls. 3/27Standing
Parsvanatha, Asthal Bohar

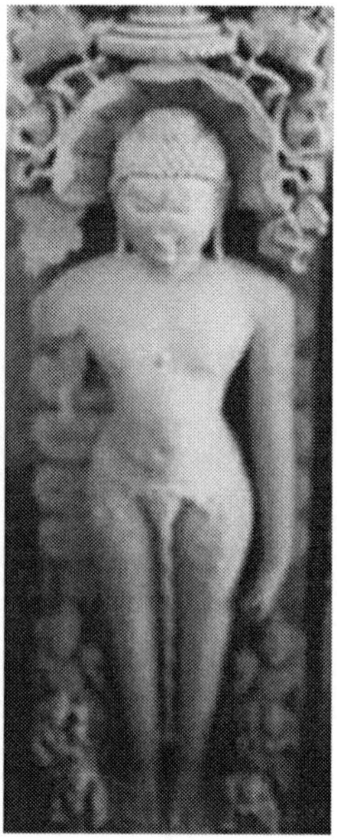

Pls. 3/28 Standing
Parsvanatha, Asthal Bohar,

Pls. 3/29 Tirthankar, Asthal Bohar

Pls. 3/30 Prasvanatha, Majara

Pls. 3/31 Prasvanatha, Majara

Pls. 3/32 Chakresvari, Ranila

Pls. 3/33 Adinatha, Ranila

Pls. 3/34 Adinatha, Jind

Pls. 3/35 Mallinatha, Narnaul

Pls. 3/36 Parshvanatha, Badhara

Pls. 3/37 Mahavira, Badhara

Pls. 3/38 Parsvanatha, Jhajjar Museum

Pls. 3/39 Tirthankar, Jhajjar Museum

Pls. 3/40 Parikar Portion, Jhajjar Museum

Pls. 3/41 Mallinatha, Jhajjar Museum

Pls. 3/42 Tirthankar, Jhajjar Museum

Pls. 3/43 Parikar Portion, Kurukshetra University

Pls. 3/44 Close up view of the above

4

The Growth, Development and Expansion of Buddhism in Haryana

Buddhism came into being some 2500 years ago when North-Eastern India was passing through great intellectual and religious upheaval. The Vedic sacrifice became unviable in urbanized society. Instead, a new religious practice emerged such as renunciation - the abandonment of worldly life for the pursuit of spiritual enlightenment. Gautama Siddhartha (C 563-483 B.C.) who later became Buddha, the enlightened one, was the founder of Buddhism (Fig. 4/1). He claimed to have discovered certain universal spiritual facts, and the teachings he based on these became the beginning of this religion. From India, Buddhism spread throughout many areas of East Asia. By the 5th century BC North-Eastern India was undergoing considerable social and political turmoil due to downfall of older clan-based principalities and the introduction of money economy. Gautama was also born into the family of Sudhodana who ruled the country of the *Sakyas* in the Himalayan foothills. At the age of 30, disillusioned with the life of luxury, Gautama left the palace at Kapilvastu and became mendicant seeker of truth on the bank of river Nairanjna (Bodhgaya), he did meditation and gained the profound insight into the nature of human existence that made him enlightened one (Buddha). He realized that overall the lives of beings are characterized by unhappiness and frustration as a result of a misplaced attachment to their self-identity and material possessions. This causes being to engage in various forms '*Karma*'. Buddha then saw that unless human beings re-orientate their lives, they have no escape from endless cycle. Furthermore, he understood, that if one had to break the sequence of events involved in '*karma*' through insight into its dynamics it would be possible to seek '*Nirvana*', a state of peace and spiritual insight.

According to Buddha this spiritual sickness is curable by following four noble truths *(Arya-Chatvari-Satya)*, which state that life is characterized by all-pervasive unhappiness, that the source of this misery is attachment and ignorance, that this situation can be overcome, and that the way to do this is to follow the eight fold path *(ashta-anga-marga):* right view and intention, right speech, conduct and livelihood, and right effort, mindfulness and meditation. The spiritual ignorance sets off a chain reaction, which leads to rebirth with their concomitant suffering. People are unwilling to accept the fact of change and impermanence *(anitya)* because of their attachment in lives and possessions.

They behave in an unwholesome nature, *(akushala)* leading to more sufferings. Ultimately, a person is responsible for their own spiritual fate whether pleasant or unpleasant. The combination of such morality and meditation insight that makes Buddhism unique.

After Buddha's death Buddhist monks transmitted his teachings throughout India and sent missionaries in most Asian countries from Afghanistan to Japan. Large Buddhist monasteries were established in India, China, Tibet and in

South-East Asia, often with royal patronage. Many Buddhist monks came to India from China, Indonesia, and Tibet to study in Buddhist universities such as at Nalanda. The teachings also evolved over time, the development of great way (*Mahayana)* around 1st century BC which emphasized self-sacrifice and compassion. Later there emerged Tantric Buddhism, which made extensive use of complex rituals and iconography.

Although Buddhism continued to flourish in South-East and East Asia, it was largely destroyed in India and west Asia by the 12th Century AD by Muslim invaders and due to revival of Hinduism.

The capital of Magadha, Rajagrha, ruled by Bimbsara and subsequently by his son Ajatashatru, both patrons of Buddha, was an important place for Buddha who delivered many sermons on the nearby *Gridhrakuta*. Buddha's later life was spent in Saravasti, the capital of Kosala ruled by king Prasenjit. Due to its location on main trade routes, Sravasti was ideal location for spreading Buddha's teaching. The Buddha had affection for Vaisali also, the capital of Vrjji. At the age of 80, Buddha began his journey, traveling from Rajgrha. After passing through Vaisali, he dined at the house of Cunda in Papa. Falling ill, he reached Kusinagara where he passed away into Nirvana. He was cremated here and ashes were divided into eight portions, which were given to the main Kingdom of Northern India.

After Buddha's death first council was held in Rajagrha (C 482 BC) to compile and authenticate the oral teachings of Buddha. In following decades '*Sangha*' grew and flourished all over. The places associated with Buddha's life became pilgrimage centers and monasteries were built with royal support. One hundred and ten years after the Buddha's death, a second council was held in Vaisali (C 373 BC) to settle some questions related to *Vinaya*, the monastic code of conduct. In this council a split occurred in the *Sangha* with the minority *sthaviras* breaking away from the more liberal *Mahasanghikas*.

In 327 BC Alexander invaded North-Western India. After his death, a Hellenistic Kingdom was established in the area around Gandhara, Purusapura and Taxila. The ruler Menandr (C 155-130 BC) extended active support to Buddhist missionaries. Gandhara became famous art school depicting Greek influence on Buddhist sculptures and Taxila first Buddhist university as well as starting point for missionaries into Central Asia.

King Ashoka (C 268 –232 BC) of Patliputra, converted to Buddhism under Mauryan expire patronage, Buddhist Centres were expanded and Stupa's built to enshrine holly relics. He also promulgated Buddhist concepts of social welfare and tolerance by carving multilingual rock edicts and on stone pillars. He also sent missionaries to Sri Lanka, Bactria, Syria and Alexandria through overland and sea trade route.

After Asoka Buddhism underwent doctrinal diversification with the emergence of the eighteen schools, such as the *Sarvastivadins, Sammatiyas, Mahishasakas* and others in India.

The Scythians from Central Asia under king Kanishka (78-102 AD) established Kushana Empire over Northern and Central India. Kanishka called 4th council in Kashmir (C 100 AD) to resolve the differences between the eighteen schools of Buddhism. Sanchi Stupa was also built during his period and Buddhism also got support from *Satavahana* kings of Southern India.

With the emergence of *Mahayana* at this time, importance of compassion and social responsibility was stressed through the action of the Bodhisattva, a person who dedicates his life to saving others. Lotus *Sutra*, new scriptures associated with *Mahayana* were composed. Nagarjuna (C 2nd Century AD) was the founder of the *Madhyamika* school of *Mahayana*. His teachings were further advanced by Aryadeva.

During the reign of Chandragupta I (319-335), Gupta Empire at Magadha also extended royal support to Buddhism. The Buddhist universities such as Nalanda, Valabhi, Ratnagiri, and Vikramsila were established during this period to attract students from all over India and rest of Asia.

The Buddhist centers were destroyed in North-West India during 5th century such as Taxila by Huns. King Harsavardhana (606-47), Pusyabhuti dynasty allowed many Chinese monks to visit India for study. One famous Xuan-Zang spent 16 years in India for studying Buddhism, leaving a detailed record of his travels.

The Pala dynasty was founded in 750 AD. During this period Tantric Buddhism flourished in the universities at Somapura and Odantapuri. They offered a path to enlightenment by using rituals and sexual yoga.

Tibet was a more developed Centre for tantric Buddhism. The series of devastating Muslim invasions from Afghanistan, which ended Buddhism in India, culminating in the destruction of nalanda university in 1199 AD with the burning of its library and the slaughter of monks.

The Buddhism spread into South –East Asia accordingly. Mehindra, son of king Asoka is said to have brought (C 250 BC) monks and scriptures to Sri Lanka and founded Mahavihara monastery in the capital Anuradhpuram and subsequently Abhaygiri monastery.

In Burma Buddhism make an impact during Mon period (5th to 10th Century) especially at Suddhammavati and at Pegu.

In Indonesia, the Srivijayan kingdom, established in Sumatra (C 600 AD). *Hinyana* from India known to have been established here by the 7th century with *Mahayana* arriving shortly afterwards. Similarly, Buddhism gradually spread in Vietnam, Cambodia, Thailand and Laos through missionaries from India since 2nd century AD.

Much water has flown in Yamuna since Delhi (ancient Dhillika, Yognipura and Indraprastha) had been the capital city of Haryana. More precisely, once upon a time, this land was known as Aryavarta[1], Brahmarshidesa[2], Brahmavarta[3], Kurukshetra[4], Madhyadesa[5], Uttarapatha[6] so on and so forth. The ancient civilization born, took shape and thrived here since time immemorial.

The discovery of large number of Pre-Harappan, Harappan and late Harappan sites in Haryana[7] indicates that this region was area of attraction for human habitation, obviously, cradle of civilization in 2nd millennium BC. The son of the soil, the Aryans lit the sacred fires on the banks of the *Sarasvati, Drishadvati and Apaya* rivers in Haryana[8] and Kurukshetra battlefield experienced famous Mahabharata war. Subsequently, in fact, many decisive battles in Haryana had not only changed the course of Indian history, direction of culture and people but also movement in numerous ways.

Menander, the Greek ruler defeated the Yaudheyas around 2nd Century BC at Rohtak which was located enroute to invaders and traders. The poet Vakpatiraja refers to Yasoverman's army advancement through Srikan-ha and Kurukshetra (Gaudavaho, Verse 484) to subdued Islamic invaders. Thanesar capital city was raided in 1014 AD by Mohamud of Gazni and many other localities in this region. The defeat of Prithviraja Chauhan at Trawri or Train in 1192, Timur's invasion in 1398 and three battles at Panipat in 1526, 1556 and 1761 respectively altogether changed the fate of Indian people, land and culture.

During the first millennium (1000-350 BC) growth of cities and development of small polities *(Janapadas)* took place and Kuru was one of the sixteen *Mahajanapada*[9], *Mahasutasoma Jataka*[10] describes Kuru realm in three hundred leagues in extent, which includes Inderpattna (Indraprastha) as its capital[11]. It seems Kurushetra (region) have extended up to Ganga with its capital at Hastinapura[12]. The *Somanassa Jataka* indicates that the Kuru Kingdom held sway and extended up to Uttarapanchala, a town in Kurura – ha ruled over by the King Renu[13]. The literary and archaeological data amply suggests that Hastinapura, the Kuru capital was washed away by the floods of Ganga during the reign of Nichaksu[14] and the capital was shifted to Kausambi[15] (*Ganga Apprehite Tasmin Nagre!)* The Buddhist literature[16] clearly mentions about city Hatthinpura It seems that Hastinapura reinhabitaled during Buddha's era because Buddha is said to have visited this city[17].

The *Mahavastu* attributes sixty thousand cities to the Kuru kingdom[18] such as *Thullakao-hita, Kammasadamma, kundi* and *Varanavata*[19].

The *Jatakas* mentions named Dhananjaya Koravya and Sutasoma. The reigning dynasty belonged to Yudhi-hila gotta, family of Yudhish-hira[20], Kuru chief Koravya is said to have paid a visit to Ra-hapala, son of a Kuru magnate, who had become a disciple of the Sakya sage[21]. It appears the Kururash-ra including the territory between yamuna and Ganga with capital at Hastinapura was originally a tract between Saraswati and Ganga, as in Mahabharata, Ganga has been mentioned as one of the seven subsidiary river of the Sarasvati.

Kuru *dhamma* was popularly known and famous which emphasis on the growth of agriculture and cultivation of moral conduct.

The '*Samantapanchac*' region was developed by Kuru's and land became 'Bahudanyaka'. The culture thrived therein was worthy of emulation by humanity all over the world. Obviously, Buddha delivered sermons of high order to convert the people of this land to Buddhism.

Buddha's visit and its influence in Haryana

The culture of Haryana was known for moral excellence and wisdom. Buddha traveled in Haryana himself to elevate the people spiritually through sermons and teachings. The *Mahavastu* and *Digha-Nikaya* texts amply describes how Buddha himself influenced the people of Kuru tribe and converted them to Buddhism[22]. The Vinaya of the *Mulasarvastivadhins* refers to Buddha's long journey along with Ananda from Hastinapura to Rohitaka via Mahanagara, Srughna, Brahmanagrama and Kalanagara[23] and from there to further Gandhara and Uddiyana and back with Yaksha Vajrapani[24]. These places such as Rohtak, Sugh near Jagadhari are clearly identifiable and Buddhist remains have also been discovered from there. Brahmangrama near Rohtak (Brahmanwas) has also been identified correctly and a broken portion of Kanakmuni image in Padmasna posture was also found from this village. O.P. Bhardwaj has identified Mahanagara with Indraprastha and Kalanagara with Kalanaur near Rohtak[25]. These places require through archaeological investigation and exploration to corroborate literarily data. *Dipavamsa* refers to Buddha's visit to a city located in the Kuru country where he received alms on the bank of the *Anotatta* lake which he crossed[26]. The Kurukshetra may be identified this place, in case, Satapatha Brahmana is (IX 5.1, 4) [27] reference is accepted about Anotatta lake as Anayatahplaksha. The Buddhist remains have also been discovered from Kurukshetra, if deemed so Thullako-hita and Kamnasadamma find repeated references in the Buddhist literature where Buddha used to stay during Kuru country journey. Buddha delivered numerous sermons at these places[28].

Thullako-hita was the seat of the contemporary kuru king, Koravya, and had a beautiful garden called Migachira nearby. Asvaghosha gives us the Sanskrit version of the name as Sthulakosh-haka and records the initiation of Rash-rapala, a saint of a local Vaisya family, by the Buddha[29]. His religious discussion with King Koravya have been narrated in the Ra-hapalasutta[30], Ra-hapala is described to have converted the Kuru King and his parents to Buddhism and as having contributed some verses to the theragatha[31]. The Madhuratthavilasini alternately spells the name of the town a Thullaka-hita where the two Brahmans, Bhadrasala and Vijitamitra, along with their family adopted Buddhism. In

Pali this place has been used as Thullako-hita. Buddhaghosha has explained that town was prosperous market-place surrounded by fertile and affluent country plentiful in grains filled in stores of inhabitants[32]. Bhardwaj has identified Thullako-hita with thol-kurri on the road from Ambala city to Kurukshetra via Jhansa while D.C. Ahir of the view that Sthanesvara is thullakao-hita. Thul Kurri is ancient site which yielded Painted gray ware (PGW) and other antiquities but archaeological excavation will settle such problems.

Kammasadamma location has been stated on ancient trade-route where Buddha used to stay usually during his visit in Kuru-desa. It was a town of considerable size and has been called Mahakammasadamma also[33].

The town has been named as Kalamsha-damma in the Divyavadana[34] and Buddhacharita[35] the town is explained to have been named Kammasadamma in the Jayaddissa Jataka because it was here that Bodhisattva, once born as a son of Jayaddissa of Kampilla, subdued his other son called Kammasapada on account of a wound (Kammasa) on his foot (pada), who under the evil influence of a Yakshini had became a cannibal[36]. The name is also attributed to the place, as it was here that the Bodhisattva Sutasoma, son of Koravya, tamed the Yaksha Kalmashapada[37]. Buddhaghosha refers to the place as Kammasadhamma and says that it originated from the initiation of the demon Kammasa into Kurudhamma[38].

Buddha had delivered many discourses here: Satipa-hana sutta, Magandiya Sutta, Ananjasappaya Sutta, Mahamidana Sutta, Mahavstipa-hana Sutta etc. one discourse each on the religious topics of the Samyutta-Nikaya and Anguttara – Nikaya was also delivered here[39]. The Magandiya Sutta tells us that during one of his visit to the Kuru country, the Buddha stayed in the Agnishala of Bhardwaja brahmana and converted the Brahmana magandiya to his faith after a protracted discussion[40]. The famous nuns Nanduttara and Mittakalika belonged to Kammasadamma[41].

Therigatha, which forms part of the Khuddaka-nikaya, contains stanzas of *Nanduttara* and *Mittakali*, of Kuru-ha. The traditional mention of the names with the lives of the Bhikshunis 'nuns' is preserved in the commentary of Dhmmapala known as the Pramatthadipani, ascribable to the 5th century A.D.

Both the theris 'female recluses' belonged to the Kammasadamma 'nigama' corporation in the Kuru country. Nanduttara, belonging to a Brahmana family, had earlier been initiated to Jainism.

Imasmim Buddhapada Kururattha kammasa damma nigme brahmana-kule -----------

Jamabusakham gahetva bhadda
(Therigatha, p.63)

This town has not been identified yet properly, however variously associated with Kamaspur[42], Kaithal[43] and Kamoda[44] but no archaeological relics are available from these places.,

During one of his journeys from Bhaddiyanagara to Savatthi, Buddha is said to have passed through Anguttarapa, Apana, Kusinara and Atuma[45]. Bhaddiyanagara (Pali) is known as Bhadrankara (Sanskrit) also.[46] The vinaya of the Mulasarvastivadins tells us that it was the capital of the republic of the Bhadra tribe where the Buddha has converted Mendhaka[47]. The name figures in other texts also and has been equated with Sakala (Sailkot), Bhakra, etc.[48] These places were certainly located in the northern region. The archaeological site at Bhadra (Distt. Hanumangarh, Rajasthan) may perhaps be identified with the Bhaddiyanagara. Anguttarapa has been equated with Aggalapura and is described to have fallen on Revata's way also during his journey at the time of the second council. This town also occurs in Tche Mang's journey from Sakala to Rohitaka. The Chinese version of the name A-kia-Lou-to may be rendered as Sanskrit Agroda or Agrodaka mentioned in the Mahamayuri[49]. It has been identified with Agroha in Hissar Distt. Przluski has observed that "The Chullavagga proves that before the editing of the vinaya, that is to say probably before the beginning of our era, the capital of the udumbaras and the city of Aggalapura were recognized as the capital of Buddhism in the North-Western regions". Agroha was important Centre of Buddhism in Haryana during historical period. Rohitika also occurs on Buddhist itineraries. Divyavadana mention it as great and prosperous city[50]. The same text narrates the Buddha's visit to Srughana (Sugh) where he won a Brahmana Indra who boasted of having no equal in beauty and learning[51].

Bodhisattva is said to have once been born to the chief queen of the Kuru King Dhananjaya in his capital Indrapatta. Bodhisattva followed Kurudhamma and brought peace and prosperity to his family[52]. Kuru king Mahendra dedicated his life to wait upon a Buddha[53]. Truly speaking Buddhism could not be a flourishing movement in Haryana up to the time of the early Mauryas – Chandragupta and Bindusara. The King Ashoka patronized Buddhism and placed it on a prominent position in India and abroad.

So far Haryana is concerned Buddhism could not take off accordingly and effectively as happened in other parts of the country during this period.

Iconography, art and architecture of Buddhist monuments in Haryana

The places connected with the four principal events of Buddha's life, viz. his birth, enlightenment, first preaching and decease, which took place respectively at Lumbani, Bodhgaya Sarnath and Kasia, were looked upon with greatest sanctity. To these were added four other places also, intimately associated with his life, viz. Srarasti, Sankasya, Rajagriha, and Vaisali, which together with the first four were regarded as the eight holy places (ashta-mahasthanas) celebrated alike in Buddhist lore as well as art. It is but natural that those places should be adorned by devout Buddhist with shrines, Stupas and Monasteries. Further according to tradition king Ashoka (273-32 BC) opened the eight out of the ten original Stupas enshrining the body-relics of the master and distributed them into eighty four thousand Stupas which he is said to have erected throughout the length and breadth of his vast empire.

Asoka is credited with the authorship of three principal type of monuments, viz., (1) Pillars, (2) Stupas and (3) Rock-cut caves.

The Stupa originated as a piled-up burial-tumulus and constituted the most characteristic monument of Buddhist religion. Symbolizing the decease (parinirvana) of Buddha, the Stupa came to be looked upon as an object of Buddhist cult-worship by the time of Asoka. Stupa were of three types and were built either to enshrine the body-relics (Saririka) or the personal effects (paribhogika) Buddha and Buddhist saints or to commemorate spots and events of religious significance (Uddesika).

The Stupa was a solid structural dome (anda), usually raised on one or more terraces and surmounted by a railed pavilion (Hermika) from which rose the shaft of the crowning umbrella (Chhatra). The Stupa had circumambulatory passages (pradkshina-patha) which were usually enclosed by railing (Vedika). The earlier Stupas were hemispherical in shape with a low base, while the later ones assumed an increasingly cylindrical from with a well-developed drum. (Pls. 4/1)

Fa-hien who visited India during the Gupta period refers to the existence of Buddhist establishments on both side of river Yamuna[54]. The Chinese pilgrim Hsuan Tsang, makes specific references of Asokan Stupas. He gives Thanesar account.

"To the North-West of the city, 4 or 5 li is a Stupa about 300 feet high which was built by Asoka raja. All the bricks are of the yellow red colour, very bright and shinning; within is a peck-measure of the relics of Buddha. From the Stupa is frequently emitted a brilliant light and many spiritual prodigies exhibit themselfes"[55]. The description of the Stupa seems to be factual and true. Not properly in Thanesar at present but one have been located near the Aujasa Ghat near the Sarasvati river". There is a mound consists of bricks of yellowish or reddish colour. Cunningham had remarked "It is probable that the smaller mound may be the remains of the Stupa from which the large pieces of the bricks have been carried away and the larger mound may be the ruins of an extensive monastery"[56]

But, the mound surveyed by Cunningham has completely vanished now. The remains of a Stupa and monastery near Harsha - ka –Tila on the bank of Sarasvati nala were traceable in Thanesar alongwith one brick masonry square tank, measuring 6 mts. size of Kushana period. We are not certain about it whether this one is the same Buddhist establishment which was seen by Chinese pilgrim or some other. Due to urbanization above relics has also been disappeared now. In fact, Buddhist remains at Thanesar appears to have been devastated due to human vandalism and Turkish onslaught. One more Buddhist monastery referred to by Yuan Chawang, located between Sannihita tank and Kurukshetra-Kaithal is not traceable now from where one Terracotta casket was found some time ago. This was demolished in 1972 to built a new strucure[57].

The Buddhist literature refers one more place in Haryana i.e. Su-lo-kin-na which rendered in Sanskrit translation as Srughana (Sugh). It was situated 400 li on North – East direction from Thanesar and subsequently Chinese pilgrim visited this place [58] Srughana has rightly been identified on the bank of Yamuna as Sugh near Jagadhari [59]. It was very big Buddhist establishment at Sugh as confirmed by Yuan Chwang account of this site. "To the South – East of the capital and in the West side of the Jumna outside the east gate of a large monastery was on Asoka tope at a place where the Ju-lai had preached and admitted men into his church. Beside this, tope was one which had hair and nail relics of the Ju-lai, and round about where some tens of topes with similar relics of Sariputra, Mudgalaputra, and other great arhats"[60] Sariputra and Maudgalayayana had predeceased Buddha and Stupa are said to have been raised over their corporeal remains. The followers of Buddha even during his lifetime raised Stupas and enshrined hair and nail pairings of Buddha. Such practice was in tradition as referred by some scholars[61]. In fact, some Stupas at Sugh may modestly attributed as a pre-Buddhist tradition relics. Similar to Piparhwa inscribed vase, a ivory casket of one inch in height, was discovered from Sugh mound (Pls. 4/2). It contained paste-like white material, resembles exactly in shape as to Piparhwa (Pls. 4/3) but without any inscription on it. This is definitely a reliquary containing the corporeal remains of Buddhist dignitary. An ivory bead from Sugh, similar to the shape of Piprahwa relic casket is of equally archaeological significance. It is 21mm in height and 17mm in diameter having vertical groves on pot-bellied portion. It suggest obviously that symbols significant to Buddha's life or depicting any events thereof were highly venerated and in use abundantly by the believers of Buddhism. Hence, such discovery from Sugh are historically eminent. Sugh was a flourishing state during 6th-5th century BC also so visited by Buddha himself. This fact has been confirmed on the basis of archaeological data available to us[62] and its mention by Panini "After the Buddha's decease the people of this country had been led astray to believe in wrong religions and Buddhism had disappeared". Observes Yuan Chwang[63]. During the reign of Asoka Sugh again became one Praiseworthy Buddhism centre and adorned by tens of Stupas and monastery. The Asokan Stupa as mentioned by Chinese pilgrim appears to have been washed away by the floods of river Yamuna.

One more Stupa located at a distance of 5 k.m. North-West of Sugh, at Chaneti (Pls. 4/4) and built by Asoka has also been referred by Chinese pilgrim out of those tens of topes. The ancient coins were found from Chaneti by Cunningham[64]. It appears Sugh and its neighborhood were under deep impact of Buddhist, philosophy teachings and phylum obviously, due to Buddha's visit in this region. Large number of Buddhist monuments were constructed here and Buddhist art flourished therein during Asokan era- under royal patronage.

One more remnant assigned to Mauryan period, originally constructed of yellowish-red colour burnt bricks, measuring 30X30X7 and 30X15X7 cm in size has been found 100 mts. South – East of village Chaneti by the side of the tract to Buriya. The texture, shape[65] and size of this Stupa fully corresponds Buddhist Sastric texts on construction and without any ambiguity resembles to Asokan brick Stupas such as Bharbut, Vaishali, Shahpur and Dharmarajika at Taxila. In all probability this is the Stupa precisely of Mauryan era, which was subsequently seen and described by Yuan Chwang one of those tens of Stupas at Chaneti.

The Mauryan pillars in Haryana : - A symbolism in Buddhist art

Sacred pillars are common to all ancient cultures. The pillars were worshiped as the image of the world axis (mundi) and are related with Cosmogony. The Asokan pillars represent the socio-cultural ethos and altruistic ideas.

The installation of chunar sand stone colossal columns by Asoka in his empire near Stupas was a new experiment in mesonic art. Such pillars were installed near Stupas and some times called Chaitya-Yupa *(Chaipya Yup Shatanikita:)* Mahabharata, Aronyaka, 2.229. The Mahavamara also ascertain the same fact. *(Haretwa Hi Tahi Yup -------Silayup---- Suti)* (Mahavmsa, 28, p220) Although this was an ancient tradition. The Atharva Veda (XIII 1.47) depicts yupa as stambha, the pillar holding the universe in form of divinity. The supreme divinity or the creator has been called purusa. (Vastusar Upanishad Chap. IV, 17')

The bull has been described in Yajurveda as the symbol of Dharma. Atharvaveda Paippalada Samhita describes the bull as symbol of virility so it is Dhamma. Therefore, a pillar with bull capital is also called Pitra-yupa. Similarly chakra is again a symbol of cosmic order (rita). The circular chakra (wheel) is constant motion symbolized time and also Brahmanda.

It appears that sole purpose of erecting pillars was not, to inscribe inscriptions, but to installed them as sacred symbols or as the cosmic pillars of the universal *Dharma*. It seems that in Buddhism old symbols acquired now meaning. Beside this, old symbology and philosophy remained influential in the mind of the artists who were inspired by the existing indigenous traditions.

The Asokan pillar majestically stands on a three- storied structure in Firoz Shah Kotla complex at Delhi was brought by Sultan Firoz from village Topra situated on Jamuna, 10 k.m. South-West of Jagadhari [66]. (Pls. 4/5)

The pillar bears the minor edicts of Asoka and an inscription of king Bisal Deva [67] of Chauhan dynasty. The recent excavation at Hansi has revealed 2200 coins of Chauhans rulers, which suggests that Tomars and Chauhans were the masters of entire Punjab and Haryana region during medieval period, precisely 8th to 10th century AD.

One Asokan pillar presently standing near Gujri mahal at Hisar and Cunninghum had copied eight fragmentary inscriptions from upper portion of this pillar [68] (Pls. 4/6) Capt. Bird had also recorded the importance of this pillar in 1838. He had rightly assumed it to be a la-pillar erected by Piyadasi. The inscription as mentioned above are not readable now but Mauryan polish (Vajralep) over it is still preserved Cunninghum and Prinsep refers that originally this pillar was located in Hansi [69] Devendra Handa is of the view that Hisar pillar was brought from Agroha which flourished as famous Buddhist Centre [70], I explored architectural members, pillars, brackets, capitals and other material of stone re-used in Hisar fort as well as in Gujri Mahal. The Hansi architectural material (8th to 10th Century A.D.) was easily available to Sultan Firoz that too nearby, instead of Agroha. However, it remains an open question to scholars who, in future may settle the issue. The Agroha was visited by Buddha and subsequently by Jivaka and Tche mang also a later period[71].

The Mauryan pillar which stands in courtyard of Idgah at Fatehabad (Pls. 4/7) resembles with Hisar pillar. There is no Asokan inscription on it, and would have been disappeared due to its constant exposure to sun and rain or chiseled off for incising arabesque records which bespeaks the Genealogy of Firoz Shah. Be it as it may, both Asokan pillars in Haryana are important antiquarian remains of Mauryan period, which were installed near Buddhist Stupas/Monastery with similar idea and faith as visualized for entire domain of emperor Asoka. The Fatehabad pillar also seems to have been transported from elsewhere nearby place. Davender Handa has suggested its original place as Agroha or Kunal but in absence of ample archaeological and historical data nothing could be determined certainly. Truly speaking, the area under reference requires a systematic exploration work on the pattern of village-to-village survey, then only, such historical problems may be settled forever on the basis of archaeological data. Last but not least, it appears that three pillars ofAsokan era existed in Haryana, may be more, if iconoclast devastation would not have taken place in this region. The Buddhist settlement were plundered and put on fire, precisely, during Sultanate period. But when other cities or town in India are compared, the numbers of Asokan pillars are fairly good in Haryana.

The Discovery of Buddhist remains from Haryana: (Buddhist images,_Stupas & Viharas)

The Sunga rulers were believers of Brahmana Dharma, obviously Buddhism lost royal patronage. However, Pushyamitra sunga has been described as a prosecutor of Buddhist according to Buddhist texts. Hence, during Sunga era also Buddhism remained unabated and simultaneously Buddhist art and architecture continued to flourish in Haryana.

Both Buddhist and non-believers subject remained in complete harmony and co-existence, keeping in view *Chakravartin* concept of the monarks. Buddhism amalgamated various folk duties such as Yaksha's, Nagas, trees which symbolized powers of fertility and rainfall. In Buddhist text, Buddha has been mentioned halting at the Yaksha-chaityas while on journey. Thus, Yaksha's and Yakshini generally found mentioned and formed integral association in Buddhism. The Yaksha's and Yakshinis were invariably found depicted on railing pillars of Buddhist Stupas[72]. One such broken sculpture of a Yakshini was discovered from Mehrauli near Qutab Minar during 1912 and presently housed in National Museum, New Delhi (Pls. 4/8). Stylistically Yakshini is datable to 2nd century BC and decorated par-excellence, if compared to other sculpture of Yakshainis from Sachi and Bharhut. It is noteworthy here that during Rajput rule Delhi enjoyed status as capital of Haryana *(Deshodesit Haryanakhya: --------Dhillikhakya ---- Nirmata)* (Epigraphia India 1.93)

Another one upper portion of a red sand stone sculpture from Palwal, presently housed in State museum Lucknow was discovered in 1914 (Pls. 4/9). Although partly eroded but without any ambiguity it is a Yaksha figure similar to other Yakshas found from Mathura and nearby region. Iconographically, this may be assigned to the early Sunga period, circa 2nd century BC. In all probability this sculpture was associated originally with Buddhist architecture in Haryana.

The most ornately carved two red sandstone pillars were discovered by D.B. Spooner from Amin situated at 8 k.m. south of Kurukshetra (Pls. 4/10). Paleographically as well as stylistically both pillars have been dated to 2nd century BC. The Amin's pillars have close resemblance with contemporary Sanchi and Bharhut stone pillars[73]. The presence of female grove on top of them suggests unequivocally that originally both were surmounted with sculptures or functional indentendently. Traditionally, Amin's association is attributed to epic Mahabharta[74] battlefield site where Abhimanyu met his heroic death.

An amorous couple of Yaksha and Yakshini is carved standing in nich. Iconographically, from toe to head both have been profusely decorated with ornaments, typical dress of the contemporary age and master pieces of art work in Haryana. The pillars are carved *Sarvatobhadra* (all four sides) depicting endulating tendrils, flowers and architectural design of delicate nature, par-excellence beauty in Indian art. Similarly second pillar has also depicting standing Yaksha figure (Pls. 4/11). This Yaksha may be compared to Sanchi gateway Yakshaa. Floral design particularly lotus are shown coming out from founal (from the mouth of crocodile) as well as Ghatpallava are marvelous. Both the pillars bears inscription in Brahmi script. R.C. Agrawaal has deciphered the epigraph as " Bhikhunika Potasa Matu danam, (the gift of the mother of a person named) Rasi (Rishi) Mitra, the grandson of Bhikhuni (a female Buddhist mendicant).

These pillars are uncomparable in richness of motifs and delicacy of art to any Sunga relics from rest of India. Be as it may, they have important bearing on the ancient art of the Kurukshetra region[75].

During the Sunga period Buddhism spread in Southern Haryana as evident from the discovery of railing pillars from Hathin which is situated 16 k.m. South-West of Palwal in Distt. Faridabad. A Yaksha figure standing in Samapada Sthanaka-Mudra has been found from Hathin carved out on it[76] (Pls. 4/12). Iconographically, Hathin's railings post are class art work of sculptures produced in Haryana. The mortise holes made for fixing crossbars into them suggests that originally these railings were architectural member of Buddhist Stupa. The upper portion of the post has carvings depicting queen Maya's dream in a medallion (Pls. 4/13). Maya sleeping on a couch, descending of elephant from the heaven to enter the Queen's Womb as seen by her in dream and other description of the story has been carved out faithfully in low relief. The scene not only represents contemporary architecture but also social-cultural standpoint. This is unmistakably an antiquity of circa 2nd century BC, highly influenced under Mathura school of Art where such sculpture were produced in white spotted red sand stone. A few letters in Brahmi (Pa da pi ki ni u)[77] are engraved on its side. The skilful craftsmanship, delicacy of sculptural art and depiction of Buddhist culture exhumated from Hathin unequivocally suggests that the railings post of Hathin, at once upon a time were originally installed in a very big Stupa. In near future perhaps archaeological operation may be more helpful for further research at Hathin.

One more noteworthy railing post of Stupa was discovered from Bhadas, situated nearby 19 k.m. North – East of Firozpur Jhirka towards Nuh. Like Hathin, Bhadas post is also located on an ancient mound. The front face of the pillar has been carved out with a standing Yaksha figure (Pls. 4/14). The face of the Yaksha is found mutilated. Iconographically, this is a perfect sculpture with all ornaments, drapery and as usually shown in the company of mythical animals. Stylistically, this is a work of 2nd century BC[78].

Buddhism became common man's faith during 2nd century BC. The Nagasena[79] thera (Monk) converted Indo-Greek king Menander in Buddhism who patronized it whole hearted. But inspite of all direct evidence of Buddhism during the reign of Menander from Haryana has not been exhumated so far. In fact, Indo-Greek coins of Menander period have been obtained from Haryana, places like Karnal, Ambala, Sugh and Rohtak etc. Hence, singular discovery of railing post from Bhadas is of great archaeological importance and suggests about construction of a Stupa during Sunga period at Bhadas.

A fragmentary railing pillar (Pls. 4/15) depicting contemporary life, a fragmentary frieze, may be part of an architrave and Triratna (three jewels) an auspicious symbol in Buddhism representing the Buddha; *Dharmma* and *Sangha* all were discovered from southern Haryana. All above objects are presently housed in Gurukula Museum, Jhajjar. The railing pillar without any ambiguity belongs to Buddhist architectural remains. The second fragmentary frieze as suggested by Devendra Handa do not seems to be a Buddhist relics. The Simha-yala alongwith three human figures, carved in relief on a flat slab of stone (central one holding garland in both hands) in no way depicted any association with Buddhist iconography and are unidentified (Pls. 4/16).

The second symbols of Buddhism such as *Triratna Dhamma, Stupa, Chakra,* Tree (Bodhi tree) etc. were considered venerated and highly regarded by the Buddhist. In fact, these symbols were under worship and auspicious. It is sometimes stated by scholars that such symbols were depicted before the emergence of Buddha images. *Triratna* is also similar type of symbol supporting Buddha in an aniconic form. The Dhamma chakra on it has been placed majestically in a graceful manner. The discovery of *Triratna* which is finished delicately and in fully evolved form, furnishes evidence of aniconic Buddhist worship from Haryana about two thousand years ago. *Triratna* symbols not only represents classical era of Buddhist art in Haryana but also its early beginning in this region.

Kanishka was great patron of Buddhism. Since Haryana formed part of his dominions Buddhism flourished here accordingly. Mathura and Gandhara were two famous school of art during this period and centre of relgion. Hence, partly broken piece of *Triratna* from Jhajjar museum is a masterpiece of Buddhist symbol discovered from Haryana (Pls. 4/17).

The folded legs portion of a Buddha image of Kushana period was found from Brahmanvas (Pls. 4/18) village in Rohtak district which is made of white spotted red sand stone from Mathura.

It bears an inscription in early Kushana characters of Brahmi as "Buddha Kanaka-muni'. In Buddhist texts Brahmanagrama found mentioned and presently also inhabitated by Brahman community. It suggests that Brahmans of the village Brahmanvas adopted Buddhism who were sivate originally.

One more broken image (torso of Buddha, presently housed in Jhajjar museum) was discovered from the same district [80] (Pls. 4/19). It is also made of white spotted red sand stone (Mathura school of art) and depicturing all *Mahapurusha-Lakshana* of Buddha. Stylistically, it is dateable to early Kushan phase and carved slightly rough.

Similar to preceding image of Buddha one more sculpture of Buddha from Agroha has been reported by Jonna Williams [81]. It is also preserved in the Jhajjar museum. The Buddha image stylistically has been carved on white spotted red sand stone and belongs to Mathura school of art. It is noteworthy that Agroha was an important centre of Buddhism in Haryana which flourished continuously being situated on ancient trade route.

In July, 1883 the Lahore Museum acquired (S.No. 389 of the Register I Register of Additions, 1867-1903, pg.65) one Buddha (seated posture) sculpture. It is also made of red sand stone and was discovered from the village Ahrwan, 5 k.m. from Palwal, Faridabd Distt. The reference of Lahore museum (No. H 671)[82] cited by Devender Handa 'Buddhism in Haryana' and the image has been stated preserved in Lahore museum. A Bodhisattva head from Mohmudpur [83] is another very important Buddhist relic (Pls. 4/20). Iconographically, the head of Bodhisattva is master piece, carved out of white spotted red sand stone and beautifully finished.

One more head of Bodhisattva was recovered from Mustafabad, Distt. Amabla during 1965-66 [84]. It was finished in Gandhara school of art Iconographically, and significant Buddhist relic from Haryana so far Gandhara style images of Buddhist art is concerned.

The most beautiful sculpture of seated Buddha, finished in Gandhara school of art was recovered from Jhajjar again.[85] (Pls. 4/21)

It is made of slate stone depicting Buddha's hands in preaching posture. Iconographically, it is a perfect sculpture where Buddha has been shown alongwith diminutive figures, Bodhisattvas, Maitraya, Apasaras and other decorative theophany relief. The art of Gandhara school is fully visible in this icon. The discovery of Gandhara Buddha from Jhajjar unequivocally suggests that Buddhist mendicants were in frequent movement on ancient trade route passing through Rohtak right upto Gandhar region.

A tablet found from Lalpur[86] (Pls. 4/22) (Rohtak) made of white spotted red sand stone depicting precise form of a Stupa is very important relic of Buddhist art in Haryana. It appears to be an architectural part of a shrine, probably Stupa wherein such small pieces are invariably carved in low relief for decoration purpose.

It seems that during Kushana period a Stupa may have existed at Bhuna near Fatehabad. The architectural pieces of railing pillar made of white spotted red sand stone was discovered from Bhuna[87] (Pls. 4/23). The pillar not only display architectural style of the age but also exhibits contemporary lifestyle and socio-cultural behavior of the people. The couples as usually found on such railing pillars are shown in different pose and life seems to pulsuate in them. Characteristically, the pillar belongs to Kushan period and a masterpiece of Indian art. It is not merely a dead stone but virtually a source of various information also related to art and architecture once upon a time flourished at Bhuna. The archaeological excavation at Bhuna mound may reveal more data about size and shape of the original Stupa along with other antiquarian remains.

Devendra Handa discovered the remains of Kushan period Stupa at Asandh (ancient Asandivat)[88] in Distt. Karnal. Asandh has been mentioned in the Brahmanas sutras, Asht-adhyayi, Mahabharata and many other texts, and must have been an important town of ancient India. Locally known as Jarasandha-ka- tila, was originally a gigantic structure of 25 mts. height which subsequently revealed a Stupa. It is constructed of bricks and may have been similar to the Dhamekh Stupa of Sarnath as evident from the exposed section of the Stupa. The plan, shape and size of Asandha Stupa appears to be extraordinary and indication of an important relic of Buddhist remains.

Some remains of Kushana period Stupa were noticed near 'Referral Hospital' at Kurukshetra a few years ago. But all has been completely demolished recently due to human vandalism. Hence, except burnt bricks of Kushana period, pottery and a few other antiquarian remains nothing is visible at site.

Since, Kurukshetra was a famous centre of all religious activities highly venerated place, the Buddhist might have chosen *Dhammashetra* Kurukshetra best suitable centre for propagating Thagata's teaching.

The ancient ruins of Rohtak city popularly known as *Khokhra Kot* has yielded a pillar capital of Kushana period (presently in National Museum) (Pls. 4/24-25). It is carved on white spotted red sand stone depicting tow seated winged lion heads on either side with monolithic body. One couple as rider has also been shown on other face of the pillar capital[89]. It could have been associated with more Buddhist remains discovered by M.D. university, History Department such as railing pillars, cross bars and coping stones from the same spot indicating the existence of a Stupa at site. It suggests that Buddhist established themselves at Rohtak and culturally played important role in this region.

Hiuan Tsang have referred five monastery at Sugh village. Remains of a monastery belong to Kushan period was exhumated South-West of Sugh village[90]. The exposed structure gives an idea about the shape and size of the monastery where Buddhist monks lived together and preached Buddhism. Sugh has been found mentioned in various texts as one important Buddhist Centre. Devender Handa has identified one Asvamukhi Yakshi of terracotta from Sugh as an object associated with Buddhism. But some more data is required for proper iconographic identification about this terracotta object.

Devendra Handa has again identified one Kushan terracotta figure from Sugh as Bodhisattva. But, iconographically his identification requires further confirmation in absence of more details about the image.

The Buddhist texts such as Divyadana [91] and various others mentions Sirsa (ancient Sairishaka) [92] as one of the important town. A small headless terracotta figurine with both arms broken was found from Sirsa (Pls. 4/26). The standing posture of the terracotta suggests that either it is a Buddha or Bodhisattva image. Be it as it may, Sirsa was situated on ancient trade route on the bank of river Sarsvati and probably at confluence of river Drashadvati and Sarasvati. Hence, all religious activities of various sects and Dhamma flourished in Sirsa continuously.

The Kushan's in Haryana were succeeded by the Yaudheyas who worshiped Karttikeya as their tutelary deity. Rohtak was their capital and centre of power. Subsequently Yaudhedyas were also subjugated by Gupta's who followed Bhagavata Dharma. Obviously, Buddhism could not received royal patronage under their control in Haryana.

The Chinese pilgrim Fa-hien, who visited India during the reign of Chandragupta II, describes to have seen Stupa's on both sides of the Yamuna [92] but about the Haryana he has not mentioned any particular site. It appears that he visited Sugh, which was a flourishing town and important Buddhist centre. Devendra Handa has suggested that a bloodstone bead discovered from Sugh depicting Chinese alien features has probably commemorate the visit of Fa-hian. But, nothing could be stated firmly on the basis of this bead alone and more archaeological data is required.

The Cunningham had observed that Tushararama or the Tushara monastery was originally situated on the hilltop at Tosham[93]. Moulded bricks of Gupta period has been reported from a massive structure situated on the hilltop. The famous Tosham inscription datable to Gupta period also refers to Bhikshu Jivama. But, more data is required to be very sure about it. There is one more mutilated female image of stone, presently housed in Jhajjar Museum (Pls. 4/27) with a child on her left lap, which has been identified as Hariti by Devander Handa. Hariti is believed to have been the Yakshi of Rajagriha converted by Buddha. Iconographically, the female figure depicted seated crossleged, holding child and swords on *pitha* do not suggest its firm association with Buddhism.

One clay sealing from Sugh has been published by Swami Omanand Sarasvati depicting Buddha in Bhumi-sparsa-Mudra. It has some legend, probably 'ye dharma hetu prabhavah[94]. The sealing is datable to Gupta period and suggests that even during Gupta regime Buddhism was popular in Haryana.

A small rectangular, partly broken tablet discovered from Sugh (Pls. 4/28) depicts a figure of Buddha flanking with two standing attandents.

This antiquity may be dated and assigned to the Gupta period. Such more pieces have been stated discovered from Sugh, sometimes with traces of Brahmi legend. The Buddhism remained intect at Sugh during Gupta age and Sugh as its important centre.

The excavation at Agroha has yielded a beautiful terracotta head of Bodhisattva (Pls. 4/29). Iconographically all features of Gupta period are visible on Bodhisattva head and placed Agroha as one of the important Buddhist centre.

Sultan Garhi (located on Mehrauli-Mahipalpur road in Delhi) has the earliest tomb built by Iltutmish in 1231 AD.

Dr. Y.D. Sharma of Archaeological Survey of India discovered some Rajput and Gupta period architectural members of temples, railing pillar of Stupa and other antiquity embedded in the roof portion of the tomb. A large number of Hindu and Jain Temples pillars were found re-used in this tomb. The discovery of a railing pillar from this place suggests that originally Buddhist Stupa once existed in its vicinity. The railing pillar (Pls. 4/30) has been carved on white spotted red sand stone and presently housed in National Museum, New Delhi.

Buddhism once again reached in glorious era during the reign of Pushpabhuties. Rajyavardhana has been mentioned as *Parama Saugata* in Harsha's Madhuvana and Banskhera inscription[95]. In fact, during the reign of Harshavardhana Buddhism again revived and received royal patronage.

The Chinese pilgrim Hsuan Tsang who visited India during the Harsha's reign describes three Buddhist monastery with more than 700 *Hinayanists* at Thanesar[96]. He had seen Asokan Stupa here but did not mentioned about status of worship and religious use. The remains of one Stupa are still visible above the ground in the area between the *Brahma Sarovara* and the Kurukshetra university (Pls. 4/31-32). The Department of Archaeology Haryana Government has exposed these relics and discovered circumambulatory path around the Stupa and remains of a monastery. The archaeological clearance work revealed its construction in two phases i.e. Kushana and Gupta respectively.

From Thanesar, the Chinese pilgrim seems to have gone above 100 li South to Ku-hum-tu (or Ch'a) monastery, which had high chambers in close succession and detached terraces: the Buddhist brethren in it led pure strict lives[97].

Ku-hum-tu has been equated with Govinda and gokan-ha and identified with modern Gunan, situated about 25 k.m. south South-West of Thanesar between Vyasthali and Nisang[98].

The Chinese pilgrim also visited Srughana (Sugh) and saw Asokan Stupa as well as others. He saw "Five Buddhist monasteries and above 1000 Buddhist ecclesiastics the majority of whom were Hinayanists, a few adhering to 'other schools"[99]. He also refers to Harsha having secured forcible the tooth relics of Buddha from Kashmir.

The account of pilgrim leaves an impression that Buddhism was flourishing throughout the entire region from Taxila to Pundravardhana in the East and from Kashmir and Nepal to the Chola Country in the South.

At Agroha remains of a Stupa datable to Harsha's reign have been excavated (Pls. 4/33). Besides this, some antiquities associated with Buddhism were also discovered from the site.

It appears that Harsha patronized Buddhism and built Stupa's and monasteries at several places under his control.

The scenario of Buddhism altogether changed during the early medieval period in Haryana. It is sometimes stated that Buddhism disappeared from its birthplace because of the hostility of Hindus. In fact, post Harsha relics of Buddhism in Haryana are rare but not absolutely absent. The Islamic invasions destroyed non-believers shrines and converted them forcefully. This was the period of uncertainty and uneasiness. The people were badly in search of truth and clear interpretation of the religious thoughts.

Devender Handa has identified a relief from Rohtak as *Panchika-hariti* and associated it with Buddhism on iconographic ground, he has dated this image to C 8th

century AD. The relief panel depicting a standing couple. The female has been stated holding two children and male figure holding a pot but second hand in *abhaya* posture is not certainly identifiable. This could be Yaksha and Yakshini *Amibika* holding tow children Subhankar and Depankar on her lap (Pls. 4/34). Such images are invariably shown with Jain Tirthankara. In any case, since the sculpture is not complete any speculation will be a guess.

An important discovery of Buddhist relics was made from Hansi in 1982 when a head of 57 bronzes (majority of Jaina) exhumated from ancient fort[100]. Two images are definitely Buddhist origin and badly mutilated. One bronze shows Buddha in Bhumisparsa-mudra and second figure represents Bodhisattva padmapani (Pls. 4/35-36) also called Avalokitesvara. The Archaeological Survey of India excavated Hansi fort during 2003 to 2005 continuously and revealed architectural members and broken sculptures of Jaina, Shiva, Vaisnava and Sakta cult in large numbers. The most important discovery is Northern black polished ware (NBP circa 600-800 BC), which was being used by Buddhist monks generally while traveling. Hansi was also important town situated on ancient trade route and Buddhism reached up to Bamiyan through this route also.

Three stone heads of Buddha from Sanghi, Distt. Rohtak[101] (Pls. 4/37) a broken head from Rohtak proper [102], one more from Adi Badri, Distt. Yamuna Nagar[103] (Pls. 4/38) are datable to 8th to 10th Century AD. A striking feature in all above heads is common i.e. chopping off from the main sculpture. It suggests that the original images were desecrated and damaged during Islamic invasion on Buddhist centre, one more seated image of Buddha in Bhumisparsa mudra discovered from a temple at historical site Taraori (Pls. 4/39) in Distt. Karnal.

Topographically, Haryana is situated between two important centre of Buddhism and Buddhist art producing school i.e. Mathura and Gandhara. The ancient trade route, which connected Gandhara with Pataliputra. (Uttarapatha) and the South (Dakshinapatha) passed through Haryana. Obviously, this is the cause that sculptures and Buddhist relics of both the schools were found in Haryana. Simultaneously art and architecture of Buddhist monuments has been exhumated through out Haryana and Punjab as evident from archaeological discoveries at Sanghol, and other sites in Harynana. The recently excavated site Adi-Badri associated with Buddhism will be discussed under separate head of this chapter.

Be as it may, Buddhism could flourish in Haryana only during reign of Asoka. It continued to be an important religion up to Kushana also but it received good impetus by Harsha (7th century.) Buddhism never disappeared completely and remained as living religion during medieval Haryana, Rohtak, Sugh and Thanesar have been the important centre. In future archaeological data will throw ample light on complete picture of Buddhism. In fact, Buddhist circuit of Haryana should be explored and excavation carried out at important Buddhist sites extensively. This will attract cultural tourism in Haryana besides discovery of many more new Buddhist sites hitherto unknown. (Map 4/1)

Recently excavated Buddhist remains from Adi-Badri, Distt. Yamuna Nagar

Lat. 30 $^{0}27^{N}$, Lon.77^{0} 27 E an archaeological excavation and exploration was carried out at Adi Badri, Distt. Yamuna Nagar, Haryana by ASI team during 2002-03.

The excavated remains belonging to 3rd-6th century AD were taken up for conservation and structural preservation. The relics of Sharirik Stupa (3rd – 6th century AD) and Buddhist monastery of Vajrayan phase (10th –11th century AD) have been recently discovered on the bank of Sarasvati. These Buddhist monuments were on the *udgam sthal* (Pls. 4/40) of the holy river.

According to excavator of the site phase – II of period I has yielded mud Stupa (3rd-4th century AD), followed by brick Stupa in phase I of period II (5th – 6th century AD). In phase II of period II, ABR II Stupa was repaired and datable to 5th –6th century AD. Phase III of period III has been assigned for monastery complex.

ABR III mound locally known as Bhawnra has yielded *Sharirik* Stupa (mud as well as brick phase) and a Buddhist Mahavihara of the Vajrayan phase.

In period I phase II evidences of relics comprising of a set of thirteen teeth of a reverent and elderly person along with fragments of bone were found placed in chamber of stone.

From period III phase II an impressive rectangular Buddhist Monastery complex having four entrance-opening courtyard, a ritual chamber, congregation hall, etc. was exposed. The main gate has been provided with a flight of steps. One seated Buddha image in the *dharma chakra pravartan mudra* has been found insitu in the central niche. (Pls. 4/41) while second fallen image of Buddha was discovered near first niche (Pls. 4/42-46) Besides this, the excavator has claimed to discovered underground meditation chamber also.

The Sarasvati, a cradle of civilization and culture, a river as well as 'the stream of knowledge' has been still flowing through living traditions and customs in India. The ancient settlements such as Adi Badri represents concept of composite culture of *Chakravertin* where Buddhist and other religious sects lived together in complete harmony and peace in Haryana.

"Nirankar Bhajyanteke Narakaar Tathadepray!
Wayn Bhagwati Sarswantya Nirakaarn Upshamahe!!

Notes

1. Manu Smriti 11.22.
2. Ibid, 11.19.
3. Nundo Lal Dey, The Geographical Dictionary of Ancient and Medieval India, New Delhi, 1971, 3rd ed; p.40.
4. For details, see R.C. Agrawala, "Kurukshetra in Early Sanskrit Literature", Journal of Indian History, Vol. XXXIII, Part I, No.97, April, 1955, pp.85-90.
5. Manu Smriti 11.21. Also see B.C. Law, Historical geography of Ancient India, Paris, 1954, p.13.
6. V.S. Agrawala, vamana-Purana – A study, Varanasi, 1964, pp.31-32.
7. B.B. Lal and S.P. Gupta (Eds), Frontiers of the Indus civilization: Mortimer wheeler Commemoration volume, New Delhi, 1984, pp.519ff and maps.
8. Rigveda 111.23, 4.
9. Anguttara Nikaya (P.T.S.) 1.213; IV.252, 256 and 260.
10. V. Fausboll, the Jataka, London, 1963, No 537.
11. Ibid. Also no.545.
12. V.S. Agrawala, India as known to Panini, Varanasi, 1963, p.54.
13. The Jatakas, No.444.

14. Nichakshu was the son of Adhisima, and sixth descendant of Abhimanyu. Hastinapur, thus, must have been washed away long before the time of Buddha.

15. B.B. Lal "Excavation at Hastinapura and other Exploration in the upper Ganga and Sutlej basins 1950-52" Ancient India, New Delhi, Nos.10 & 11, (1954-1955), pp.147.

16. Bharata Singh Upadyaya, Buddha-Kalina Bharatiya Bhugola (Hindi), Prayaga, V.S. 2018, p.411.

17. Divyavadana, p.45. Buddha's visit to Kurudvipa is recorded in the Dipavama IV.39.

18. Bhardwaj, op. cit, p.150.

19. Raichaudhuri, Political History of Ancient India, 6th edn, Calcutta, 1953, pp. 133-34.

20. The Jataka, Nos. 413, 495 etc.

21. Majjhima Nikaya (PTS), 11, 65f.

22. Mahavastu, Calcutta ed, Vol.11 p.564; Digha Nikaya, 11.55ff.

23. M. Wintermitz, A History of Indian Literature, Vol. II, Calcutta, 1933, p.232.

24. E. Frauwallner, The Earliest Vinaya and the Beginnings of Buddhist Literature, Rome, 1956, pp.31ff.

25. Bharadwaj, op. cit., p.39.

26. Dipavamsa (Ed. H. Oldenberg, London, 1879), vv. 43-44.

27. Datta and Phadke, op. cit., p.39.

28. Ahir, op. cit., pp. 12-15. We owe much to Bharadwaj regarding the details of these two places.

29. Buddhacharita (Ed. With Hindi tr. S.N. Chaudhuri, Purnea, 1955) XXI. 26. In the Avadanasataka (Ed. P.L. Vaidya, Darbhanga, 1958. p.227), however, Ra-hapala has been described as Kuri king's nephew.

30. Majjhima Nikaya, No.82.

31. B.C. Law, tribes in Ancient India, 2nd ed., Poona, 1973, p.22; 46; Majjhima Nikaya (Ed. Jagdish Kashyap, Nalanda, 1952), Vol. II, pp. 281ff.
32. Chaudhuri, op. cit., p.31.
33. Ibid. No. 537.
34. Divyavadana, pp. 515ff.
35. Buddhacharita XXXI. 27.
36. The Jataka, No.578.
37. Ibid. No. 537.
38. Upadhyaya, op. cit., p.409.
39. Ahir, op. cit., pp. 13-1.
40. Majjhima Nikaya, II, pp. 198 ff. Magandiya offered to Buddha his beautiful daughter Magandiya in marrige but the offer was declined for obvious reasons.
41. Chaudhuri, op. cit., p.31.
42. Upadhyaya, op. cit., p. 410.
43 Ahir, op. cit., p. 14.
44. Bharadwaj, op. cit., p. 159. There is another place known as Kamash now, located on the Barara-Shahbad road, about 5 km from the former, in district Ambala. The mound here, measuring 250 X 200 X 8 metres, is partly under habitation and yields Painted Grey Ware, early historic red ware, coins, and other relics (Manmohan Kumar, Archaeology of Ambala and Kurukshetra Districts {Haryana}, Unpublished Thesis, Kurukshetra University, Kurukshetra, 1978, p. 37), but the definite Buddhist association or Buddhist relics from this site are still awaited.
45. For details see J. Przyluski, Ancient Peoples of the Punjab, Indian Studies, Calcutta, 1960, pp. 9 ff.
46. Divyavadana, pp. 77ff.
47. Vinaya, Part I (Ed. S. Bagchi), Darbhanga, 1967, pp. 145 ff.

48. For details, see Przyluski, op. cit. and Bharadwaj, op. cit., pp. 155-56.
49. Agrodake Malyadharah (line 8) and Agrodake Munjakesah (line 70) of Mahamayuri edited by Sylvain Levi in Journal Asiatique, 1915, pp. 19-138.
50. Divyavadana, pp. 77 ff. Also see Handa (1970), loc. cit.
51. Ibid. p. 47.
52. Law (1973), op. cit., pp. 28 ff. Buddhist impact on Delhi and its environs during the reign of Asoka is indicated by the discovery of a minor rock edict of Asoka from Bahapur near Lajpat Nagar, in Delhi. See also M.C. Joshi and B.M. Pande, "A Newly Discovered Inscription of Asoka at Bahapur, Delhi, " Journal of the Royal Asiatic Society, 1967, pp. 96-98, Pls. I-II.
53. Foe details see Bharadwaj, op. cit., p. 151.
54. H.A. Giles, Records of Buddhist Kingdoms, Cambridge, 1923, pp. 19-20.
55. Samuel beal, Si-Yu-Ki: Buddhist Records of the Western World. Vol. I, London, 1906, p. 186. See also Thomas Watters, On Yuang Chwang's Travels in India, Delhi, 1961 (First Indian ed.), p. 316.
56. Alexander Cunningham, Archaeological Survey Report, Vol. II, pp. 220 – 21.
57. Manmohan Kumar, "Buddhist Remains Near Thanesar, " in Gleanings of Indian Archaeology History & Culture: Prof. Dr. R.N. Mehtra Commemoration Volume, edited by K.D. Bajpai et al, Vol. I, Jaipur, 2000, p. 86.)
58. Panini, Ash-adhyayi, I. 3, 25; Patanjali, mahabhashya, III. 2, 15; Divyavadana, 74. 17, 22; Mahamayuri, 11.23 & 60; Brihatsamhita XVI. 21 etc.
59. Cunningham, Archaeological Survey Report, Vol. II, pp. 226-27; The Ancient Geography of India, Varanasi, 1963 (reprint), pp. 290-91.

60. Watters, op. cit., p. 319.
61. Debala Mitra, "Buddhist Art and Architecture – A Study", Keynote Address in Art & Architecture Section, First International Conference on Buddhism & National Cultures, New Delhi, Oct. 10-15, 1984 (cyclostyled copy), p.3.
62. Suraj Bhan, "Report of Excavation at Sugh (1964 and 1965)", Journal of Haryana Studies, Kurukshetra, Vol. IX (1977), pp. 1-49. Suraj Bhan, however, puts the earliest phase (period IA) of Sugh between 500-400 BC, which we feel should go back by a Century or two earlier as is indicated by the sherds of Painted Grey Ware found form it.
63. Watters, op. cit., p. 319.
64. Cunningham, Archaeological Survey Report, Vol. II, p. 123, pl. LVIII.
65. T.W. Rhys Davids, Buddhist India (Reprint), Calcutta, 1959, p. 37.
66. Cunningham, ASR, Vol. XIV, pp. 78-79. Also see Marg, Haryana Heritage Number, Vol. XXVII, No. 4 (Sept. 1974), pp.8-9.
67. See for details E. Hultzsch, "Delhi-Topra Pillar Edicts", Corpus Inscription Indicarun, Vol. I, Oxford, 1925, pp. 119-37.
68. Cunningham, ASR, Vol. V, p. 142.
69. Cunningham, loc. cit.
70. C.J. Rodgers, Report of the Punjab Circle of The Archaeological Survey for 1988-89, Calcutta, 1891, p.43.-
71. Przyluski, op. cit., p. 10.
72. Foe details see Ananda K. Coomaraswamy, Yaksas (Washington, D.C. 1928-31), 2 vols., Reprint, New Delhi, 1971. See also J.P. Sharma, Jaina Yakshas, Meerut, 1989, pp. 44-52.
73. R.C. Agarwala, "Sunga Pillars from Amin, near Kurukshetra, "Lalit Kala, Number 14 (New Delhi, 1969), pp. 50-52, Pls. XVI-XVIII. Also see his "Early History and Archaeology of

Kurukshetra Region, " Indian Historical Quarterly, Calcutta XXXI (4), 1955, pp. 204-06. We owe the details and illustrations of these pillars to R.C. Agrawala's description and illustration in the Lalit Kala No. 14. These pillars were smuggled from Amin to London but were brought book to India and are now displayed in the National Museum, New Delhi. the duplicates of these pillars were left by the smugglers in the Thakurji ka Mandir on the bank of Suraj Kund at Amin,.

74. Ibid.

75. R.C. Agrawala (1969), op. cit., p. 52.

76. For details see Prem Goswamy, "Two Early Kusana (?) Railing Pillars from Haryana," Journal of the Indian Society of Oriented Art, New Series, Volume XV (1985-86), pp. 1ff. & Pl. I.

77. Cf. Prem Goswamy, op. cit., p. 5 referring to Shri Krishna Deva's reading *'PADAYIKINI'.*

78. This post, too, was first noticed by Punia (1976, op. cit., p. 182 Pl. XX and 1981, loc. Cit., Figs. 3-4). Punia gives it dimensions as 190 X 26.27 cm whereas HARDAMA records rightly show them to be 149 X 24 cm. Prem Goswamy (op. cit, p. 3) has also followed the dimensions of HARDAM.

79. T.W. Rhys Davids, The Questins of King Millinda, Sacred Books of the East Series, Vols. 35-36, Kshemedra's Avadana-Kalpa Lata also corroborates it. (Ibid. Vol. 36 p. XVII).

80. Sheela Devi, op. cit., p. 207, Pl. XXXII.C.

81. Joanna Cottfried Williams, "An Ardhnarisvara-Linga, " in Kusumanjalai : New Interpretation of Indian Art & Culture (Sh. C. Sivaramamurti Commemoration Volume), edited by M.S. Nagaraja Rao, Vol. II, Delhi, 1987, p. 299.

82. Saifur Rahman Dar, "Fifty years of Research in Gandhara Art (1947-1997)", in Buddhism and Gandhara Art, edited by R.C. Sharma and Pranati Ghosal, Shimla –Varanasi-New Delhi, 2004m p. 23.

83. Sheela Devi, op. cit., p. 208, PL. XXXII. E. It is also preserved in the Gurukula Museum, Jhajjar.
84. Indian Archaeology 1965-66 – A Review, p. 82.
85. It was seized by the police from Jhajjar in November 1972 while investigating the theft of three Gandhara images from a temple near Jhajjar.
86. Made of fragile kankar stone, it measures 39 x 32 cm, and is now preserved in The Department of Archaeology and Museums, Haryana (HARDAM). It bears Index No.1/352.
87. It was procured by us for HARDAM while serving as Deputy Director during 1984-85.
88. Devendra Handa, "Identification of Asandivat" Vishveshvaranand Indological Journal, Hosiarpur, Vol. III, Pt. Li, (Sept., 1965), pp. 278-81.
89. R.C. Agrawala, "Some Kusana Sculptures in the National Museum, New Delhi and Allied Problems," Bulletin of Museums and Archaeology in U.P., No.3, June 1969, p. 19-20 and figs. 10-11.
90. Suraj Bhan (1977), op. cit., pp. 3-4.
91. Divyavadana (Ed. P.L. Vaidya, Darbhanga, 1959), 256:
92. Giles, op. cit., pp. 19-20.
93. Cunningham, ASR, V, p. 140.
94. Saraswati, op. cit., No.476.
95. Epigraphia Indica, Vol. I, p. 72; Vol. IV, pp. 208ff.
96. Watters, op. cit., p. 314.
97. Watters, op. cit., p. 316.
98. Ibid. ; Cunningham Ancient Geography of India, p. 290. See also R.C. Agrawala, "Early History and Archaeology of Kurukshetra and Ambala Division," Indian Historical Quarterly, Vol XXXII (1), March 1956, p. 33.
99. Watters, op. cit., p. 318.

100. Devendra Handa, Jaina Bronzes from Hansi, Shimla-New Delhi, 2002, pp. 32-34, Pls. 59-61.

101. Silak Ram, op. cit., p.223, Pl. XXVI. B. it is now preserved in Gurukula Museum, Jhajjar. It measures 25 X 17.5 cm.

102. HARDAM. Index No. 1/115. A Buddha image is said to have been found from here in the lst Century (Journal of the Asiatic Society of Bengal, 1881, p. 72). Rodgers had also seen an image of Buddha near the tank of Gokarna (rodgers' Report, p. 74.). A Buddha head is enshrined in the Sitala Mata Mandira near gokarna ka Talab and worshipped as Siva now.

103. It is now preserved in the Department of Ancient Indian History, Culture and Archaeology, Punjab University, Chandigarh. Buddha in padmasana and dharma-chakra-pravartana-mudra datable to circa 11th – 12th centuries from this site have also been noticed by Manmohan Kumar (1978), op. cit., pp. 148, 163 and 288, Pl. XVI. C and B respectively.

Pls. 4/1 Sanchi Stupa

Pls. 4/2 Sugh

Pls. 4/3 Piparhwa

Pls. 4/4 Chaneti Mound

Pls. 4/5 Asokan Topra Pillar

Pls. 4/6 Asokan Pillar, Gujari Mahal

Pls. 4/7 Asokan Pillar, Fatehabad

Pls. 4/8 Yaksi, Mehuralli

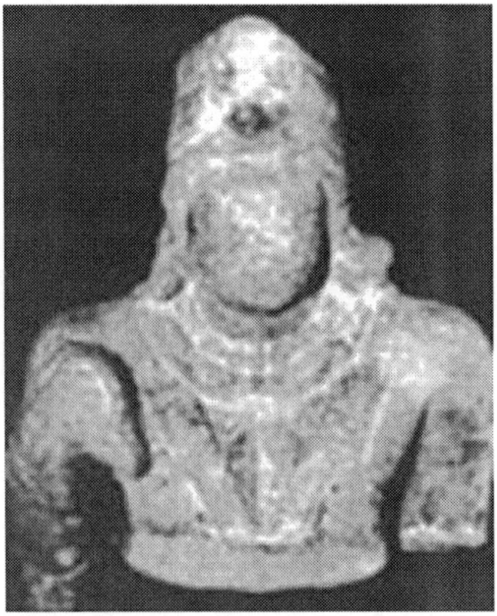

Pls. 4/9 Yaksa, Palwal

Pls. 4/10 Railing Pillar, Amin

Pls. 4/11 Railing Pillar, Amin

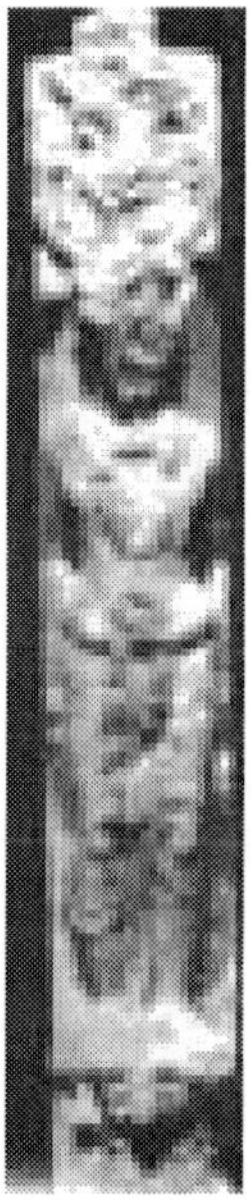

Pls. 4/12 Railing Pillar, Hathin

Pls. 4/13 Maya's dream, Hathin

Pls. 4/14 Railing Pillar, Bhadas

Pls. 4/15 Railing Pillar, Jhajjar Museum

Pls. 4/16 Fragmentary Frieze, Jhajjar Museum

Pls. 4/17 Triratna, Jhajjar Museum

Pls. 4/18 Kanakamuni, Brahmanvas

Pls. 4/19 Buddha, Jhajjar Museum

Pls. 4/20 Bodhisttva, Mohmudpur

Pls. 4/21 Gandhara Buddha, Jhajjar

Pls. 4/22 Tablet, Lalpur, Jhajjar

Pls. 4/23 Railing Pillar, Bhuna

Pls. 4/24 Pillar Capital, Rohtak

Pls. 4/25 Pillar Capital, Rohtak

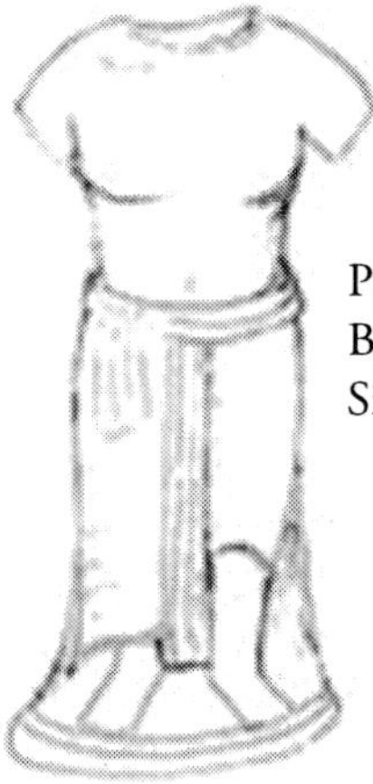

Pls. 4/26
Bodhisattva,
Sirsa

Pls. 4/27
Unidentified

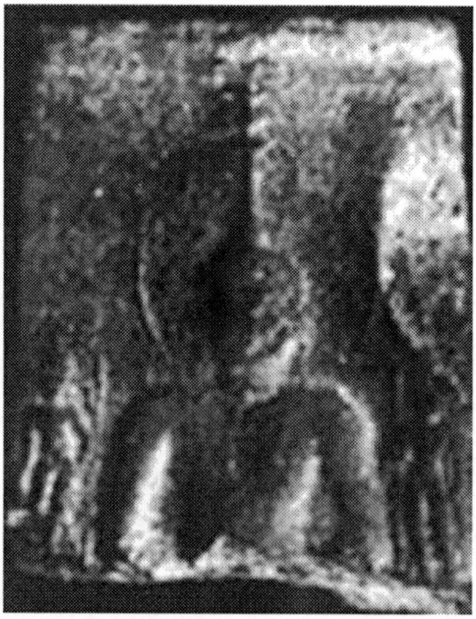

Pls. 4/28 Tablet, Sugh

Pls. 4/29 Bodhisattva, Agroha

Pls. 4/30 Railing Pillar, Sultan Garhi

Pls. 4/31 Stupa, Brahma Sarovara

Pls. 4/32 Stupa, Brahma Sarovara

Pls. 4/33 Stupa & Monastery, Agroha Sarovara

Pls. 4/34 Yaksa & Yaksibu

Pls. 4/35 Budhha, Hansi

Pls. 4/36 Padmapani, Hansi

Pls. 4/37 Budhha, Sanghi

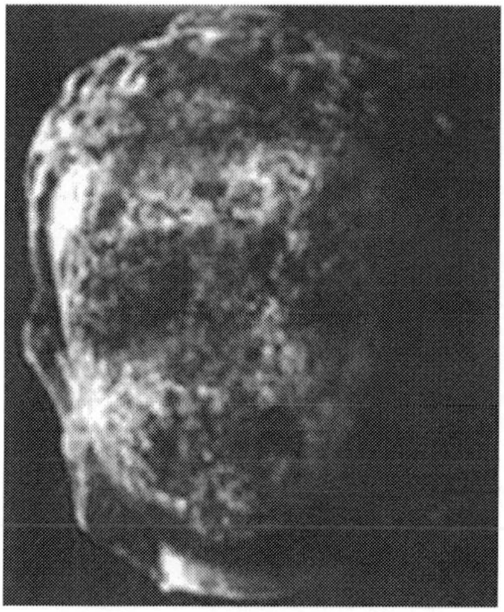

Pls. 4/38 Budhha, Adi Badri

Pls. 4/39 Budhha, Tarori

Pls. 4/40 Udgam Sthal, Sarasvati

Pls. 4/41 Buddha, Adi Badri

Pls. 4/42 Buddha, Adi Badri

Pls. 4/43 Buddha, Adi Badri

Pls. 4/44 Pillar, Adi Badri

Pls. 4/45 Monastery, Adi Badri

Pls. 4/46 Buddhist remains, Adi Badri

5

Retrospect and Conclusion of the Study

Linguistically, reference from Rigveda of '*Varuraja*', in context of Haryana is quite significant. The word *Varu* (in Vedic Sanskrit) or *Baru* (Corrupt form of Sanskrit) in Haryani or Hriani dialect derived from same, means 'full of greenery' (Bahudhanyaka). This is how, the word *Baru* grazing ( ) has been still in vogue in Haryani dialect since then.

The '*Varuraja*' (raja or rajye (reign)) has been suffixed which denotes, 'the land, area, reign) full of greenery, hence, this region of Kururastra was named Harayana (Haryana).

This land of Kurus had also the privilege of being the home of Indian spiritual thoughts. Tradition has it that the region was blessed by the teachings of Buddha, Mahavira, Guru Nanak and many others.

This is the region where eight fold ethical conduct (*angamahadharma*) of austerity (*tapes*) truth (*Satya*), forgiveness (*Ksama*), Kindness (*Daya*) purity (*Sancha*), Charity (*Dana*) yoga and continence (*Brahmacharya*) was cultivated.

Both the master, Buddha and Mahavira visited Haryana with a view to guide the people of this country whose *'Kurudharma'* became popular all over among *Sodasamahajanapadas.*

The historical remains of human activities in Haryana can be made out from the discovery of the Palaeolithic stone tools from Pinjore at the foothills of Himalayas and Firozpur Jhirka in the Aravalis. The excavations and exploration conducted in Haryana have revealed that it was inhabitated as early as 3000 B.C. The remains of Harappan culture or Indo-Sarasvati culture are found in Haryana all over which has been confirmed by archaeological excavations at various sites and explorations carried out on the ancient banks of Sarasvati, Drishadvati, and other rivers in Haryana. The Aryans have been stated to kindled the sacred fire on the banks of above cited rivers. The discovery of painted gray ware (PGW)C 1100-800 BC has been associated with Mahabharata era by some scholars and large number of its sites yielded painted gray ware.

In the later times, the realm of the Kurus divided into three parts i.e. Kuru – Jangala, Kurudesa and Kurukshetra. However, many people of this region seems to have well received the Buddhist and Jainism philosophy and religion during the time of Mauryas as evident by the discovery of Asokan pillar edicts and Stupas and Viharas from Haryana. The Jain images alongwith architectural parts have been discovered from many sites which suggests that Jainism also flourished in Haryana between 7th to 12th Century AD. The important centre of Jainism were at Hansi, Agroha, Pinjore, Rohtak, Asthal-Abohar etc.

In fact, both ancient trade route passed through Haryana, hence, the invaders and traders followed them regularly. During Saka, Kushana and Yaudheys era various religious, sects and philosophy took shape and thrived here in complete harmony and coexistence. Be that as it may, Saivism and Hinduism (Sanatan Dharma), according to personal belief, remained important religion in Haryana constantly.

The imperial Guptas under Samudragupta, the powerful ruler between 325 to 350 AD patronized art and culture and considerable progress was made in various fields including literature. The Huns invaded Haryana during Sakandagupta's reign and ruled for some time. But soon emerged a powerful dynasty of the Puspabhutis of Thanesar. Harshvardhana ruled from Kurukshetra and Kanauj as his capitals whose reign may be considered a significant epoch in the history of Haryana. Subsequently, Pratiharas, Tomars and Chahamana ruled Haryana till invasions of Muslims and finally whole India came under them after the death of Prithviraja at Tarori in Haryana.

Inspite of the fact that the region was repeatedly devastated Haryana retained its cultural economic and social identity intact. The traces of Kurudharma are still preserved in rural Haryana even now, because traditions never die in India. If, Buddha and Mahavira born today, they will recognized Haryana immediately, Haryana has not changed much.

Large number of sources – literary, archaeological, and accounts of foreign travelers are available which speaks a lot about political, economic, religious life of the contemporary Haryana through the ages.

The archaeological remains have been discovered belonging to Jainism and Buddhism in Haryana from various villages/sites. Two Jain images from Dhana (Patan

Sehar) Jhunjnu, 13 sculpture from Mohanbari, one head from Sanghi, Buddhist sculpture and pillars from Hathin, Bodhisattava from Saga (Karnal), Dharmachakra from Khokhrakot, antiquity from Kilayat (Kaithal), sculpture from Brahmanvas (Kankmuni), Kaniska's coins from Bodo, Buddha's seal from Sugh, Jain images from Badli (Jhajjar), Buddha sculpture from Naurangabad (Bhiwani) terracotta head of Bodhisatttava (8th century AD) from same site, remains from Jhajjar, Chaneti, Asandh, Thanesar, Topra, Nimana mound near Kalanaur, and literature from Jain temple Hansi, besides, bonze sculptures, Jain temple Sonepat, Jain temple Gohana, Two Jain temples from Rohtak (Bara Bazar and Sarai Mohalla), Danapatra (Buddhist relics) presently in M.D. University Rohtak, inscription on a temple in Baund village, Buddhist relics from Adi-badri, antiquity from Aharva near Palwal, sculptures from Pinjore, Jain images from Jahajpul (George-bridge) Hissar, Black stone sculpture from Akbarpur (Barohta), images from Beri, Jahajgarh and Kasali, Jain sculprture presently housed at Ambala cant in a Jain temple, and many Jain and Buddhist architectural parts in various museums in Haryana represents a fairly good picture of both, religious activities and impact respectively.

Buddhism flourished in Haryana during Asoka era due to royal patronage. The Kusan Kings also supported Buddhism and subsequently Puspabhutis provided support to Buddhist establishments. Archarya Shankar tuned down Buddhism and finally Muslim invasions devasted it from Haryana.

Jainism made fairly good progress in Haryana and many Jain temples were built during medieval period (7th to 12th Century AD). The Hansi, Pinjore and Agroha were its important centre while Rohtak, Asthal-Abohar and various other sites yielded Jain sculptures. The Jain Archaryas composed many literary works in Haryana and guided inhabitants to follow true path of peace and non-violence. Both sects of Jainism i.e. Svetambara and Digambara flourished in Haryana.

I conducted field survey of villages and sites. In fact, organized archaeological village-to-village survey and documentation of field data is essentially required to represent a clear picture related to Jainism and Buddhism in Haryana. Large numbers of sites have not been reported faithfully. The problem oriented excavation work on some selected sites will throw ample light on research project work in future.

The antiquity of Jainism is older then Buddhism. The influence of Jainism in Haryna, has been found reflected in various literary works from the time of Buddha even. But, Jainism could not attained popularity in this region as Buddhism achieved, obviously, due to royal patronize. Both sects i.e. Svetambara and Digambara of Jainism never became mass religion of Haryana as in case of Saivism or Vaisnavism. Although it has been stated that Rohidays (Rohtak) was blessed by several visits of Mahavira, according to literary traditions. In any case main centers of Jainism were Agroha, Pinjore and Hasi. Subsequently, till the rise of Pratiharas, Tomars and Chahmanas (8th – 10th Century AD) Jainism remained under low profile in Haryana. After 10th Century AD. Jain Acharyas like Jinesvara Suri, Jinavallabha Suri, Jinachandra Suri traveled extensively and preached tenants. Jinavallabha composed literature on history and various aspects of Jainism. These Acharyas chose

Haryana and Rajasthan to propagate Jainism and established Vidhichaityas which continued to flourish in Haryana till the advent of Islam.

The archaeological remains dateable to 8th – 10th Century AD has been found from various sites in Haryana including architectural parts and sculptures etc. The Majra village near Rohtak has yielded many Jina images during excavation. The Jain relics discovered from Haryana belongs to classical age and master pieces of Indian art.

As far as Buddhism is concerned in ancient Kurudesha, the Mahavastu attributes 60 thousand cities to Kuru Kingdom but place names such as *Hatthinipura, Thullakotthika, Kammasadamma, Kundi and Varnavata* are only a few, which finds mention in Buddhist literature. Buddha himself visited Haryana for preaching his dharma. According to Mahavastu and Digha Nikaya the master himself converted the people of the Kuru tribe. As mentioned in Mularravastivadins Buddha visited Surughana (Sugh) Brahammangrama (Brahmanvas) Kalanaur, and Rohitak in Haryana. Mahavastu narrates many Buddha's visit at Thullakotthita, (Sthulakostnaka (Thanesar), and Kammasadhmma (Kamaspur) in Haryana. Dipavamsa and Mahamayuri (Buddhist texts) refers Buddha's visit to a city in Kuru country (Kurukshetra), Agrodaka (Agroha) where master is said to have stayed during his journey from Bhadranaka to Sravatthi (Sravasti).

The Haryana had been visited by many Buddhist monks and Sthaviras. But, according to Buddhaghosa not a single monastery was built in Kuru country during Buddha's life time. It refers Buddha's stay in a Brahmin's house outside Kammasaddama. It appears that upto Mauryan period no monastery or Stupa was constructed in Haryana. Asoka built many Stupas and a few of them are in Haryana.

Fa-hien visited Haryana during Gupta period and saw many Buddhist establishment of Asoka on both side of Yamuna. Hieuntsang who visited Haryana during Harsha's period also saw Asokan Stupa at Thanesar. Three Asokan pillars, Stupa at Sugh, Thanesar and Chenati suggests that Buddhism progressed in Haryana during Asokan era.

The Indo-Greek king Menander was converted to Buddhism by Nagasena, who ruled Haryana during 3rd – 2nd Century BC.

Kanisk (1st Century AD) was great patron of Buddhism. The discovery of Buddha and Boddhisattva images from Haryana belonging to Kusana period are masterpieces. Agroha and Asandh have remains of Stupas of Kusana age. The railing pillars of Hathin, Bhuna, Bhadas, Lalpura, Amin further confirms existence of Stupas during Sunga-kusana period in Haryana. Newly excavated site Adi-badri has also yielded Buddhist monastery and images.

During Yaudheyas era Buddhism declined in Haryana. The Gupta rulers were mainly Bhagavats, hence, Buddhism, obviously tuned down under them.

The Puspabhuti's again patronized Buddhism and Rajyavardhana has been mentioned as Param-Saugata. During reign of Harsha's Buddhism received impetus again in Haryana. Yuan Chwang saw Buddhist monastery at Thanesar where 700 Hinayanists were residing.

After Harsha's death Buddhism declined in Haryana and practically disappeared from the land. Alberuni stated' the whole of western Asia was Buddhistic before the advent of Islam'.

Thus, Buddhism could flourish in Haryana only during the reign of Asoka and continued during Sunga, Indo-Greek, Saka and Kusana period. It received good impetus by Harsha during 7th Century AD. It, however, continued to be a living religion during medieval period. The Muslim invasion devasted Buddhism from Haryana completely.

Truly speaking, Haryana is full of cultural wealth and eagerly looking for intensive archaeological reconnaissance. The scholars from Haryana will certainly revealed it's glorious past devotionally, thus *Pratankirtimpavarnu.* The learned world expects so from Haryanvi's.